I0816200

CHRISTIAN PATRIOT

12 WAYS TO CREATE ONE NATION UNDER GOD

TAYLOR MARSHALL

A POST HILL PRESS BOOK
ISBN: 979-8-89565-185-8
ISBN (eBook): 979-8-89565-186-5

Christian Patriot:
12 Ways to Create One Nation Under God

Cover design by David D. Thomas

All quotations of the Bible are from the Douay-Rheims 1899 American Edition unless otherwise noted. All Psalms are quoted as numbered in the Septuagint and Vulgate Psalms ordering unless otherwise noted.

This is a work of nonfiction. All people, locations, events, and situations are portrayed to the best of the author's memory.

Post Hill Press
New York • Nashville
posthillpress.com

Published in the United States of America
3 4 5 6 7 8 9 10

To my eight children, who are my strength and my joy.
Patriots to their Pater and their Patria.

TABLE OF CONTENTS

TABLE OF CONTENTS

FOREWORD
by Harrison Butker

What a blessing it is to be alive in this day and age. God has chosen us to be His soldiers at this very moment of existence in a war that has already been won. It is this sentiment that I am constantly coming back to for encouragement. When I worry about society's future and how it may negatively affect myself and those closest to me, I remember that I simply have to show up. I must do my part and know that even in the confusion and failures that may come, God is present and has not abandoned us. In *Christian Patriot,* Taylor Marshall eloquently lays out what our country requires to truly achieve one nation under God. Will we do our part and embrace the role of a Christian Patriot? God is in control, we simply have to say yes.

After completing eight seasons in the NFL with a historic franchise, winning three Super Bowls, experiencing seven years of marriage, and welcoming three children into this world, the first thirty years of my life have surpassed any expectations I could have imagined. Most men don't get married until thirty, most families don't have three or more children, and only around 0.023 percent of high school football players make it to the NFL. I know what you're thinking—getting to the NFL is statistically harder to do than the other two, obviously. But believe it or not, my beautiful family is what I am most proud of.

I'm so thankful God gave me the grace to say yes to getting married young and yes to serving a large family.

With the responsibilities of being a husband and father, I am constantly reminded of my shortcomings since my actions, or lack thereof, directly affect the well-being of those under my care—my wife and our three children. Even if you are not a man or are not married, you can most likely find someone or something that relies on you for its care. No matter how small our responsibilities may seem, God has placed us there for a reason, and we can embrace our situation and improve upon our mistakes by growing in virtue. The Christian life ideally mirrors the steps of Christ and strives to move past our fallen nature to conquer our flesh. Christ says the spirit is willing, but the flesh is weak. How can we overcome the temptations of the devil, the world, and ourselves if not by developing virtue and subjugating our flesh?

Beyond my duties as the head of my family, I've been given a platform as an NFL player, and I always try to discern what I should do with it. There are many decisions to be made, but I have to remember my platform is for God and His glory. With that in mind, it makes all those minute decisions a lot easier. As a Christian, I firmly and wholeheartedly believe that Christ is King and that we must use our talents and treasure to further this truth and to say yes whenever we can to defend it.

If I were to go through the journey of how I got to this point in my beliefs, it would include many people and events. One person it would surely include would be Dr. Taylor Marshall. I first encountered Dr. Marshall on YouTube while watching some of his educational videos on the scriptures and the traditions of Catholicism. I remember reading on his website about the virtues and trying to learn as much as possible. When he started commenting more on the Church hierarchy, it was intriguing to me—especially as someone who was proud of the traditional teachings of the Faith but somewhat confused by the actions of the hierarchy that was leading it. I found it comforting to hear explanations of why we were where we were and how we got there. In 2019, I had the pleasure of appearing on his show to talk about my time on the Kansas City Chiefs. We then reconnected four years later and have had a relationship ever since.

Taylor Marshall is a gentleman who encourages the praying of the rosary and surely leads so many souls back to Christ or introduces them to the Holy Mother Church for the first time. He's someone that has promoted the Latin Mass and brought about its awareness to so many. I'm thankful for his *Bible in a Year* reading schedule and his resources provided by the New Saint Thomas Institute (NSTI.com). I'm most grateful for his example as a husband and father and to behold the fruits of his marriage with Joy—his beautiful children. He is a man of humility, a man who loves Our Lord and His Church. I'm thankful for my friendship with this great man and thankful for his example in his personal life and work.

I pray God blesses this book and opens its readers' hearts to fight for Christ as King of this great nation. May we say yes to growing in virtue and accepting our duties as Christian Patriots. I'm thankful to be alive right now. This is the time that God has destined for us to be on earth, our time to be saints. May we be a light of Christ to those around us and impact our world in all that we do for God's greater glory by recognizing and not wasting the talents God has given us. Let's do the most challenging part and say yes to being present in the upcoming battles. Let's pray for our leaders, for our president, for the future of this country, and for wisdom and guidance from our Lord. He will never fail us and of course, He has already won. God Bless America.

To the Heights,
Harrison Butker

CHAPTER 1

WHY ARE CHRISTIANS LOSING THE CULTURE WAR?

"They get bitter, they cling to guns or religion or antipathy to people who aren't like them or anti-immigrant sentiment or anti-trade sentiment as a way to explain their frustrations."[1]

—Barack Obama, April 11, 2008

Muslim countries have Muslim laws, culture, rules, and customs. Israel has Jewish laws, culture, rules, and customs.

India has Hindu laws, culture, rules, and customs.

However, if a Christian nation with a Christian majority attempts to promote Christian laws, culture, rules, and customs, it faces strong resistance.

Why?

Take a look at your high school classroom, college campus, public library, courthouse, social media, or streaming services. What do you see?

1. LGBTQ+ ideologies.
2. Social Justice Movements like BLM, Antifa, etc.
3. Critical Race Theory and Social Marxism.

4. Christian business owners are fined and imprisoned for not violating their morals.
5. Demand for chemical castrations and transgender surgeries for youth.
6. Drag Queen story hours in schools and public libraries.
7. Books depicting detailed accounts of degenerate sex acts.
8. The defense of abortion up until birth, during birth, and even opposition to the Born Alive Act allows doctors and nurses to deny medical care for a baby that survives abortion.
9. Satanic and occult imagery depicting Lucifer, Baphomet, and horned goat idols as well as public religious recognition for the Church of Satan.
10. Hollywood films, music, and television shows that mock Christianity while promoting the secular work agenda and anti-Christian values. Sex scenes, homosexuality, and using the name "Jesus Christ" as a curse is ubiquitous.
11. Preference for the religious liberty of Judaism, Hinduism, Islam, and atheism over Christianity.
12. Sexualization of minors and demand for lowering the legal age of sexual consent.
13. Efforts to redefine the traditional family by promoting deviant lifestyles as better and equal.
14. Political movements to remove parental rights in decision-making about their children's gender, health, and education.
15. Christian Churches are vandalized or burned down without investigation or recourse.
16. Christian churches, organizations, and pro-life groups and persons are being persecuted and imprisoned.

The cultural ethos of Christianity and Natural Law is under attack and taking a beating. Some have concluded that we are living in a "post-Christian" society, but the book in your hands rejects that label. We are not "post-Christian" because we have not lost the culture war...yet.

This book is a declaration that "Western Civilization" is merely a modern euphemism for "Christian Civilization," and that Christian Patriots must defend, sustain, and extend the reign of Jesus Christ in their hearts, in their families, and within the political arena.

This current culture war for *Christian civilization* (let us stop referring to it as "Western civilization") is more consequential than the First and Second World Wars combined. Sadly, Christians are currently losing this war, but this is only temporary. "But in all these things we overcome, because of him that hath loved us" (Romans 8:37). Our Lord Jesus Christ conquered sin, death, and hell. Christ sits victorious on his throne and has already declared: "I make all things new" (Revelation 21:5). The key to this renewal of all things in Christ lies in the prayer he taught us: "Thy Kingdom come, Thy will be done, on earth as it is in Heaven" (Matthew 6:10). His grace is sufficient and effective for us, but we must pray for it and live for it—not only for the sake of His kingdom, but also for the salvation and well-being of our children and our children's children.

If we are currently losing the culture war, we must begin with an honest self-reflection of why we are losing. What deficiencies in our Christian worldview allowed this to occur? What compromises did we make in the 1950s? That analysis begins with our infernal enemy: Satan.

THE DEVIL CONVINCED THE WORLD HE DIDN'T EXIST

"The greatest trick the Devil ever pulled was convincing the world he didn't exist."

—*The Usual Suspects* (1995)

In his harrowing demonic dialogue *The Screwtape Letters,* C.S. Lewis depicts the devil's conundrum of whether to remain hidden or visible to humanity. The demon "Screwtape" describes his cruel dilemma to an inferior demon:

> Our policy, for the moment, is to conceal ourselves. Of course, this has not always been so. We are really faced with a cruel dilemma. When human beings disbelieve in our existence, we lose all the pleasing results of direct terrorism, and we make no magicians. On the other hand, when they believe in us, we cannot make them materialists and skeptics.[2]

"For the moment," the demon explains, "we conceal ourselves." The same Luciferian strategy is revealed in the plot of the Academy Award-winning film *The Usual Suspects,* which won the Oscar for Best Screenplay in 1996. The treacherous villain Keyser Söze remarks, "The greatest trick the Devil ever pulled was convincing the world he didn't exist." C.S. Lewis and Keyser Söze were not the first to identify this tactic of the devils. The earliest known description of it was by the 19th-century French poet Charles Baudelaire, who stated, "The greatest trick the Devil ever pulled was convincing the world he didn't exist."[3]

The horrific bloodshed and cultural destruction of the First and Second World Wars provided ample evidence that Lucifer and his fallen angels prowled the world, seeking the ruin of souls. I propose that the demons immediately shifted their strategy in the post-war 1950s. They retreated into hiding to wait for the right moment to reveal themselves once more.

CHRISTIANS ACCEPTED THE LIE

Christians, through no fault of their own, embraced a terrible lie after the Second World War. By appealing to the "separation of church and state," the socialist infiltrators of the 1950s proposed a Faustian deal with the devil that sounded like this:

> Regardless of our personal beliefs, we are reasonable people of goodwill. To prevent future wars, we must set aside our ideologies, dogmas, and convictions. You Christians should take your Christianity out of public discourse, and we can proceed with a civil dedication to the common good. After all, there's the "separation of church and state," right?

Unknowingly, Christians shook hands with the devil, signed the deal, and then tucked away our faith. Tacitly, we agreed that the Holy Bible, the Ten Commandments, and the teachings of Our Lord Jesus Christ would from now on become a "private matter." Our retreat from the public square and the privatization of our Christian faith created a significant vacuum waiting to be filled. Beginning in the 1960s, that vacuum was filled. A cultural revolution ignited within the dry kindling of the 1950s' perceived spiritual neutrality. The spark transformed into the inferno of what we now call the "New Secular Religion."

THE NEW SECULAR RELIGION

If the greatest trick of the Devil was to convince the world he didn't exist, the second greatest trick was to persuade everyone that his "New Secular Religion" isn't really a religion. This is Satan's master plan. Secularists argue that no religion, including Christianity, the largest and most influential religion, can publicly influence or direct political discourse or policy. Yet these secularists established their religion while asserting, "Our worldview is not a religion!" Next, they impose that worldview on every single citizen.

When students study comparative religions, they examine systems of belief, holy days, rituals, ethics, temples, and clergy in relation to each religion's affirmation of their deity or deities. The New Secular Religion asserts that it has no faith and no god at its core. However, it acts as a cult, displaying all the characteristics of a world religion. They have their dogmas, their feast days, their processions, their rituals, their morality, their monuments, and their appointed clergy. Additionally, they follow a policy of shame, exclusion, persecution, and inquisition. Anyone who dares to question their dogmas, defy their leaders, or refuse to bow to their totems will be treated as worse than an infidel. Here is a guide to the dogmatic vocabulary of the New Secular Religion:

1. "Excommunicated" is relabeled as "canceled."
2. "Dogma" is interpreted as "the infallible collection of woke ideologies to which one must believe for employment or inclusion."
3. "Sacraments" are the rituals that must be guarded and funded by the state, such as abortion, transgender surgeries, etc.
4. "Seminary" is now all publicly funded schools and colleges that are required to teach the dogmas and ethics of the New Secular Religion.

5. "Clergy" are the ordained leaders of NGOs, and the archbishops are those who can ascend to public office or to the boards and executive offices of major corporations. Once they ascend, they must teach, enforce, and police that the dogma is accepted.
6. "Missionaries" are the actors, influencers, and nonprofit leaders who work tirelessly to "convert" all people to their dogma.
7. "Inquisition" is redefined as the media that monitors all institutions and private citizens 24/7 for deviations from the dogmas.
8. "Justice" is no longer the pursuit of righteousness and "giving each his due" but the forced global redistribution of all material goods.
9. "God" is redefined as the "collective of woke individuals," and "Gods" are redefined as the "individuals" themselves.
10. "Satan" is redefined as the evil Christians who once enslaved and raped the world under the force of their dogmas.
11. "Salvation" is redefined as liberating the oppressed from the evil Christians who held the world in captivity.

With all this religious structure in place, they will assert that they are neither a religion, sect, nor church. If a Christian quietly shares a Bible verse or references the Ten Commandments, the New Secular Religionists react with outrage and initiate their Inquisition. You will be canceled if you refuse to recant (excommunicated from society and income).

Their greatest trick, similar to that of Satan, is convincing us that they are neither a "church" nor a "religion," when in reality, they have become the most potent cult on Earth.

CULT AND CULTURE

The New Secular Religion is, in fact, a demonic cult, whether they admit it or not. While Christians have generally tolerated other religions and refrained from forced conversions for the past 2,000 years, the New Secular Religion does not uphold religious freedom or tolerance. Their persecution primarily targets Christians. They show significantly more tolerance toward Judaism, Islam, Hinduism, and Buddhism than Christianity. Why? Christians still wield considerable influence over cultural transformation. Their infernal agenda suggests that Christians remain strong. We are not in a post-Christian era. We can reclaim ground and emerge victorious for the sake of Christ.

The influence of religion flows downstream to shape the culture of society. The term "culture" originates from the Latin word *cultura,* derived from *colere,* which means "to cultivate, to till, to tend, to care for." Originally, *cultura* referred to the act of cultivating farmland, but over time, it evolved to encompass the cultivation of the soul and society. The positive impact of Christianity resonates throughout cultures associated with Christendom. No historian can deny that hospitals, universities, orphanages, widespread literacy, public libraries, and the inherent dignity of each person created in the image of God emerged from Christian culture.

It's time for Christian Patriots to stop feeling embarrassed about their faith. The cultural advancements in the world resulted from the reign of our Lord Jesus Christ as He extends His kingdom "on earth as it is in Heaven." The only valid objection to this, even from within Christian circles, is the reference to "the wall of separation between Church and State"—a phrase coined by Thomas Jefferson in his 1802 letter to the Danbury Baptist Association in Connecticut. Before we explore Jefferson's concept of the "wall of separation," let's first consider the appropriate theological stance of the Christian Patriot as both a citizen of a country and a member of the Church. Is Christian nationalism the way forward?

CHAPTER 2

CHRISTIAN NATIONALISM OR CHRISTIAN PATRIOTISM?

In the aftermath of the contested 2020 presidential election and the events at the Capitol on January 6, 2021, a noticeable shift occurred in American conservatism. Trump's MAGA movement began to reassess what it meant to be "conservative." What are we actually "conserving"? Are we conserving values, morality, low taxes, family, or religion? Is the Constitution sufficient, or is something more needed for "conservatism" to succeed? Many lifelong conservatives reevaluated the battle lines and sought to recalibrate their political strategy. Social media, podcasts, and Elon Musk's purchase of X (formerly Twitter) allowed Christian voices to elevate "Christian values" above "conservative values." This strategic shift is often identified as the rise of "Christian nationalism."

WHAT IS CHRISTIAN NATIONALISM?

Christian nationalism is a political and cultural ideology that aims to merge Christian identity with national identity, claiming that a nation—often the United States—should be explicitly governed by Christian principles and ethics. American Christian nationalists reference the nation's founding, laws, and destiny as divinely ordained, citing Proverbs 14:34: "Righteousness exalts a nation, but sin is a reproach to any people." Supporters view Christianity as the foundation of national prosperity, frequently prioritizing policies that reflect biblical morality over pluralism, while critics consider it a distortion of faith that risks idolatry—placing the state above God.

At its core, Christian nationalism merges theology with patriotism. Sociologists Andrew Whitehead and Samuel Perry define it as "a cultural framework that promotes Christianity as essential to American civic life" (*Taking America Back for God*, 2020). It's not simply about religiosity but a belief that the nation's laws, symbols, and identity should embody a Christian ethos—such as "In God We Trust" being more than just a motto on a dollar. It often aligns with conservative politics, highlighting traditional marriage, pro-life policies, and resistance to secularism rooted in Psalm 32:12: "Blessed is the nation whose God is the Lord."

Christian nationalism has roots that extend back to colonial America. The Pilgrims, who arrived in the 1620s, viewed themselves as a "city upon a hill," merging faith with governance. The American Great Awakenings (1730–1840) ignited revivalist fervor, connecting national morality to divine favor—revivalist Jonathan Edwards advocated for repentance as a means of societal renewal. The 19th-century doctrine of Manifest Destiny framed westward expansion as God's will, aligned with American exceptionalism.

Its modern form crystallized after World War II. The 1950s saw the addition of "under God" to the Pledge amid Cold War anti-communism, framing America as Christianity's bulwark. The Moral Majority, founded in 1979 and led by Jerry Falwell, politicized evangelicals, giving rise to the Religious Right—Falwell's rhetoric that "America is God's instrument" still resonates today.

In 2022, Stephen Wolfe's *The Case for Christian Nationalism* challenged the status quo of Christian conservatism and became the manifesto for one strand of Christian nationalism. Wolfe, a political theorist from the Reformed/Calvinist tradition, argued that nations thrive when rooted in Christian principles, drawing from Scripture and influential Christian thinkers to propose that a Christian nation-state is both natural and desirable. He critiqued secularism as a destabilizing force and envisioned a government that reflects Christian values as a means to love one's neighbor and country. Similarly, Andrew Torba and Andrew Isker's *Christian Nationalism: A Biblical Guide for Taking Dominion and Discipling Nations* presents a more populist perspective. Torba, the CEO of Gab, and Isker, a Reformed pastor, frame Christian nationalism as a call to reclaim culture for Christ, advocating a dominionist approach in which Christians actively shape society according to biblical mandates. Their work emphasizes grassroots action and rejects secular pluralism.

Liberal opponents soon noticed the increasing conservative support for Christian nationalism. Andrew L. Whitehead and Samuel L. Perry's *Taking America Back for God: Christian Nationalism in the United States* (2020) contends that Christian nationalism promotes ethnocentrism, nativism, and authoritarian tendencies, which contradict their interpretation of the Christian teachings of tolerance and love. Likewise, progressive Kristin Kobes Du Mez's *Jesus and John Wayne: How White Evangelicals Corrupted a Faith and Fractured a Nation* (2020) traces the historical roots of Christian nationalism within evangelicalism, linking it to white supremacy, patriarchy, and political power. She argues that Christian nationalists have distorted Christianity into an instrument for cultural dominance instead of spiritual renewal. Similarly, Amanda Tyler's *How to End Christian Nationalism* (2024) presents a liberal Baptist viewpoint claiming that Christian nationalism contradicts Jesus' teachings.

IS NATIONALISM THE WRONG WORD?

The liberal opponents of Christian nationalism naturally want to associate Christian nationalism with Nationalsozialistische—Nazis. Nationalism need not be Nazism, but the current rhetorical strategy is to associate all "rightwing" movements as being "literally Hitler," fascist, and Nazi. The problem here is the term "nationalism."

"Nationalism" is a relatively recent post-Enlightenment term lacking traditional precedent in the Christian tradition. The concept of nationalism emerged from the French Revolution of 1789. It entered the English language around 1798 but did not gain significant recognition until the 19th century. Since World War II, nationalism has become a common term in political discourse, often evoking feelings of ethnic superiority. The origins of "nationalism" lie in the French Revolution, and its associations have been marred since then.

For Christians, the term *patriotism*—not *nationalism*—signifies the proper relationship between Christians and the government. The word "patriotism" derives from the Latin *patria,* meaning "fatherland" or "homeland," which in turn derives from *pater,* meaning "father." This root word connects patriotism to fatherhood and family, fundamental elements of culture and society. The suffix -ism denotes a practice, so "patriotism" essentially means "the practice of loving one's father and fatherland."

The word "nationalism" derives from the Latin word *natus,* the past participle of *nasci,* meaning "to be born." The term "nationalism" leans toward the passive association of "being born," whereas the term "patriotism" leans toward the active association of "loving a fatherland." Patriotism evokes the inheritance of father to child and thereby establishes the foundation for the traditional family in society. Plus, feminists hate it.

In ancient Rome, devotion to the *patria* was regarded as a civic virtue, exemplified by figures like Cicero, who lauded the love of one's country as a natural duty. Christianity later reframed this concept through a theological lens, balancing earthly loyalty to the fatherland with divine allegiance to the heavenly fatherland of "Our Father." From a Christian perspective, patriotism takes precedence over nationalism because it aligns more closely with the virtues of charity and justice.

Nationalism is absent in theological content, while patriotism boasts a rich tradition. As Saint Thomas Aquinas describes it, patriotism falls under the virtue of piety, a natural extension of honoring one's parents as outlined in the Ten Commandments.[1] It represents a love for the familiar—father, land, beliefs, and family—aimed at promoting the common good for all. Nationalism, however, often transitions from love to a form of natus-birth supremacy, prioritizing nativism. Thomas Aquinas conceptualizes patriotism as a virtue within the *ordo amoris* (order of love), which reflects a hierarchy of loves: God first, then parents, family, neighbors, and finally, fatherland.

AUGUSTINE ON THE CITY OF MAN AND THE CITY OF GOD

In the New Testament, Jesus exemplifies respect for earthly political authority while transcending it. When asked about Roman taxes, He replies, "Render to Caesar the things that are Caesar's, and to God the things that are God's" (Matthew 22:21). This teaching suggests a dual loyalty: Christians are called to honor their civic duties—implying a form of patriotism even when the government is pagan—while prioritizing their ultimate citizenship in heaven. St. Paul reinforces this in Romans 13:1, stating, "Let every person be subject to the governing authorities. For there is no authority except from God, and those that exist have been instituted by God." Accordingly, patriotism begins as obedience to a God-ordained order, provided it aligns with divine law.

Saint Augustine of Hippo, in his seminal work *The City of God*, offers a perspective to frame Christian patriotism within the Christian life. He differentiates between the "City of Man," the earthly domain of temporary societies, and the "City of God," the eternal community of the faithful. Augustine states, "Two cities have been formed by two loves: the earthly by the love of self, even to the contempt of God; the heavenly by the love of God, even to the contempt of self" (*City of God*, book XIV, chap. 28). For Augustine, patriotism is acceptable—even commendable—when it serves the common good and reflects God's justice, but it becomes distorted when it places the nation above God.

Saint Augustine saw earthly nations as provisional, flawed reflections of the divine order. A Christian patriot, therefore, loves their country not as an ultimate end but as a means to cultivate virtue and peace among its people. Augustine warns against a prideful nation. He noted how Rome's glory often concealed its moral decay. In Augustine's view, true patriotism is a stewardship of God's creation, a call to make the City of Man a reflection of the divine harmony found in the City of God. Augustine draws upon the teachings of the Apostle Peter, who described Christians as the *ethnos hagion* (Greek for a "holy nation") that derives their identity primarily from being "born of the Spirit" (John 3:6) and as citizens of the heavenly "Jerusalem that is above" (Galatians 4:26).

Saint Thomas Aquinas builds on the Augustinian foundation by integrating patriotism into his theology of virtue. As we have seen, Aquinas classifies love of country as a subset of piety, a virtue connected to the Ten Commandments' call to honor thy father and mother. "Man becomes a debtor to others in various ways, according to their various excellences and the diverse benefits received from them…and after God, man is especially indebted to his parents and his country."[2] Just as we owe gratitude to our parents for life, we owe a debt to our homeland for sustenance, culture, and protection.

For Aquinas, patriotism is not blind loyalty but an ordered love directed toward the common good—the flourishing of all persons within a society. He emphasizes justice as the guiding principle: a patriot seeks the welfare of their nation while respecting the rights of others, including neighboring peoples. However, Aquinas makes it clear that this love is subordinate to charity, the love of God above all. When national loyalty conflicts with divine law—as in the case of unjust wars or oppression—it must yield, for "we ought to obey God rather than men" (Acts 5:29).

The New Testament teaches that earthly nations are temporary and subordinate to the eternal "nation" of God's kingdom (Revelation 7:9). Patriotism recognizes this transience, loving a homeland without making it absolute. Nationalism, by absolutizing the human nation, risks turning it into an idol. Christian nationalists (who often speak from the Reformed/Calvinist tradition) have advanced the conversation by rightly focusing on God and the kingdom of Jesus Christ. They rightly embrace the biblical promise, "Blessed is the nation whose God is the Lord" (Psalm 33:12). A more comprehensive and convincing approach is to align theology and vocabulary with the Augustinian and Thomistic tradition, which centers on patriotism as a virtue. "Christian Patriotism" integrates our 2,000-year-old tradition with its strengths not only in biblical exegesis but also in Natural Law, virtue ethics, and the establishment of a multinational Christendom that encompasses a global (not globalist) perspective.

In essence, it is preferable to be a Christian Patriot (the title of this book) rather than a Christian nationalist. Christian Patriotism aligns with the Ten Commandments and the Christian theological tradition, embodying the etymological meaning of patria as a father's gift—a calling to nurture both family and homeland under God's law. Nationalism, which lacks this moral restraint, is prone to what Thomas Aquinas might refer to as an "inordinate affection" for the natural order, upsetting the balance of justice and charity. Therefore, patriotism represents the theological path that Christians should pursue. As Christian Patriots intent on incorporating Christian culture and morality in the public space, let us examine the lost history of "separation of church and state" (Chapter 3) and then "what a Christian government is" (Chapter 4).

CHAPTER 3

THE LEGEND OF SEPARATION OF CHURCH AND STATE

The abolition of Christian prayer, the Christian cross, the Christian Bible, and Christianity as *a whole* from the town square, schools, businesses, courthouses, parades, and civic life is defended by the presumed political doctrine of "separation of church and state." Christians now watch in dismay as Muslims establish Shariah courts; the LGBTQ+ lobby raises flags on every civic building in America and at our foreign embassies; and Satanists put up statues of the idol Baphomet in courthouses. When Christians are permitted to offer prayers in civic settings, they are explicitly instructed to exclude "in the name of Jesus Christ" from their prayers. All of this is justified by an appeal to the separation of church and state.

This was not the case until recently. America was founded as a Christian nation, with a Christian culture and education system. Even as late as 1960, 42 percent of schools permitted or required Bible reading, and 50 percent reported some form of daily homeroom devotional prayer.[1] Cities and towns celebrated Christian plays and parades in honor of Christmas, Saint Patrick's Day, and Easter. In 1956, Manhattan's financial district showcased three massive crosses formed by lighted windows that illuminated New York's skyline to honor Good Friday and Easter.

New York City honoring Good Friday (United Press Telephoto)

Clearly, the separation of church and state had not and did not prevent Christians from "imposing" their faith upon society. So how did we arrive at our contemporary predicament where employers regularly ask employees to take off their cross necklaces at work, while LGBT literature and books on atheism are stuffed into public school libraries?

THE WALL BETWEEN CHURCH AND STATE

My public high school history teacher enthusiastically taught our class (incorrectly) that the "separation of church and state" is a cornerstone of the American Founding. "This is why we no longer pray in school or use the Bible," she said with a smirk, "as a textbook for science or history." Her contemporary interpretation of the "separation of church and state" suggested that Christianity must be privatized and removed from political and public display. "Almost all the wars and political unrest in European history stemmed from the union of the Church and the State," she taught us. "The Crusades, the Spanish Inquisition, the Wars of Religion, and the French Revolution could have been avoided by applying the separation of church and state." No one in high school disagreed with her account. She continued to explain, "Our Founding Fathers brilliantly pinpointed this flaw in the European system. Separation of church and state brought about religious freedom, freedom of speech, and American prosperity." We nodded, accepting her class lesson as dogma.

As I grew older, I realized that her account of European and American history was inaccurate. The Pilgrims and Puritans were *not* advocates of the "separation of church and state," as their colonies enforced their religion more rigorously than the English king from whom they had fled. The colonies of Plymouth, Massachusetts Bay, Connecticut, New Haven, and New Hampshire were founded by Puritan Protestants who politically and financially supported their churches. Their theological convictions influenced their schools, laws, and courts.

PROFESSION OF FAITH FOR OFFICE HOLDERS

The unique role of Jesus Christ and Christianity in American culture and politics continued after the Declaration of Independence. All thirteen colonies mandated that officeholders and public officials be Bible-believing Christians with faith in Jesus Christ. For instance, the 1776 State Constitution of Delaware required the following oath:

> I, ______________________, do profess faith in God the Father, and in Jesus Christ His only Son, and

> in the Holy Ghost, one God, blessed forevermore; and I do acknowledge the Holy Scriptures of the Old and New Testament to be given by divine inspiration.

If an elected official refused this oath, he could not assume office. Other states contained similar Christian oaths for their public officials:

- The 1776 Constitution of Pennsylvania required officeholders to acknowledge the divine inspiration of the Old and New Testaments.
- The 1776 State Constitution for Maryland required officeholders to declare a belief in Christianity.
- The 1778 Constitution of South Carolina required officeholders to be Protestant and to accept the Bible as divine revelation. This was revised in 1790 to include Catholic Christians.
- The 1776 Constitution of North Carolina stated that no one who denied the truth of the Protestant religion could hold office. Atheists remained banned from office until 1961 when the "separation of church and state" was reinterpreted.
- The 1784 and 1792 Constitutions of New Hampshire required the governor to be Protestant.
- The 1796 Constitution of Tennessee specifically required public officials to acknowledge God and a future state of rewards and punishments.
- The 1780 State Constitution of Massachusetts required the governor, lieutenant governor, and legislators to declare belief in the Christian religion.

Where is the "wall of separation of church and state" taught to us by my high school teacher? The thirteen colonies that became the thirteen United States were explicitly Christian and required elected officials to be Christians. Moreover, many of the original colonies had adopted state-sponsored Christian denominations. One might expect that this all changed after the American Revolution or after the ratification of the Constitution. Some post-Revolution colonies disestablished their state-sponsored denominations, but many American states retained an officially established church that even received support from state taxes.

- The State of Virginia established the Anglican/Episcopalian Church until 1786 with the Virginia Statute for Religious Freedom, written by Thomas Jefferson.
- The State of Georgia established the Anglican/Episcopalian Church until 1789.
- The State of South Carolina honored the Anglican/ Episcopalian Church as the established church until 1790.
- The State of Connecticut established Congregationalism as the state-supported denomination until it was disestablished in 1818.
- The State of New Hampshire established Congregationalism as the established church until 1819. Until 1968, New Hampshire provided public funding for Protestant classrooms (but not Catholic classrooms).
- The State of Massachusetts established Congregationalism as the state church until 1833.
- The State of North Carolina did not subsidize a specific Protestant denomination, but it barred Catholics from holding office until 1835.
- Rhode Island established religious freedom for Protestants and Jews, *but not for Catholics.*

Connecticut, New Hampshire, and Massachusetts continued to honor a state church even after the First Amendment to the US Constitution, which was ratified in 1791 and stated: "Congress shall make no law respecting an establishment of religion, or prohibiting the free exercise thereof." Some states disestablished their Christian denominations from receiving political support and tax funding, but this disestablishment did not *wall off* Christianity from civic or public life.

CHRISTIANITY AS THE PUBLIC RELIGION OF AMERICA

A study of American history from 1776 until the Civil War reveals that Christianity was explicitly woven into the political and civil lives of Americans. A cursory reading of Mark Twain's *The Adventures of Tom Sawyer* illustrates how deeply Christianity was intertwined with civic life as late as the 1840s. Political speeches and presidential addresses were filled with appeals to Christianity and the Holy Bible. George Washington once said to the Native Americans: "You do well to wish to learn our arts and ways of life and above all—the religion of Jesus Christ. These will make you a greater and happier people than you are."[2] Abraham Lincoln famously appealed to Americans by asserting: "Both [North and South] read the same Bible and pray to the same God, and each invokes His aid against the other."[3] John F. Kennedy stated: "The rights of man come not from the generosity of the state, but from the hand of God."[4]

Until the middle of the 20th century, it was common practice for public schools to start with a Christian prayer accompanied by Bible readings. Many students learned to read using the Bible as their primary text. As late as 1949, Bible reading was part of the educational routine in the public schools of at least thirty-seven states. Twelve states legally *required* Bible reading in schools. In

1960, 42 percent of American school districts allowed or mandated Bible reading as part of their curriculum, and 50 percent reported some form of daily homeroom devotional exercise.[5] Christian prayer in schools wasn't prohibited until 1962 when the Supreme Court ruled that school-mandated prayers in publicly funded schools are unconstitutional.

IS THOMAS JEFFERSON THE PROBLEM?

Thomas Jefferson (1743–1826) was the principal author of the Declaration of Independence and the third president of the United States. He permanently imprinted his intellectual influence on the founding of the United States of America. Recent analysis indicates that Jefferson was not merely ambiguous about Christianity. Jefferson was explicitly opposed to Christianity and the Holy Bible.

Jefferson asserted that he regarded John Locke, Francis Bacon, and Isaac Newton as the three greatest men who ever lived. He overlooked Jesus Christ, Abraham, Moses, and the Apostles. His political philosophy was shaped by the writings of Gibbon, Hume, Robertson, Bolingbroke, Montesquieu, and especially the atheist Voltaire. These authors are linked to the Enlightenment's critique of Christianity, and although Jefferson never supported the extreme actions of the French Revolution, he drew his ideas from the same intellectual environment as the giants he admired.

Philosophically, Jefferson identified with the ancient Greek philosopher Epicurus, who lived from 341 to 270 BC. Epicurus rejected the philosophies of Socrates and Plato, founding his own school of thought in Athens in 307 BC. He taught that while the gods exist, they do not interfere in human affairs. Epicurus was a forerunner to the deistic theology embraced by Jefferson, who believed that God exists but does not have a personal relationship with humanity.

While Jefferson was raised in the Anglican/Episcopalian Protestant tradition, he famously abandoned Christianity after a careful study of the New Testament. Jefferson convinced himself that the true message of Jesus had been corrupted by the authors of the Gospels and by Saint Paul the Apostle. To remedy this corruption, Jefferson privately selected specific New Testament verses representing the "true teachings" of Jesus Christ to compile into a book titled *The Life and Morals of Jesus of Nazareth*, now known as the *Jefferson Bible*.

Jefferson omitted all references to the miracles of Jesus and excluded any affirmations of His bodily resurrection. He claimed that he had discovered the "true Jesus" within the corrupted New Testament, "as easily distinguishable as diamonds in a dunghill."[6] Jefferson's correspondence and writings reveal that he rejected the Christian belief in the Holy Trinity, the divinity of Jesus as the Son of God, and original sin. Jefferson held slaves; more controversially, he fathered children with his slave Sally Hemings while she remained in bondage to Jefferson.[7]

While Jefferson was illustrious in his own time, perhaps the time has come for Christians to reassess the status of Thomas Jefferson and his intention for the wall of separation between church and state. He was not a confessional orthodox Christian by any means. His "wall of separation" was founded on Deist convictions and Enlightenment philosophy hostile to Christianity. As Christians, we should not agree to his revolutionary terms. Every nation that has conformed to the "separation of church and state" has devolved into an atheistic and liberalized culture. Foreseeing our secular predicament, John Adams wrote forcefully against Thomas Jefferson on this matter, reminding Jefferson that Christianity was the principle upon which the Declaration was signed and preserved:

> The general principles on which the fathers achieved independence were the only principles in which that beautiful assembly of young gentlemen could unite.... And what were these general principles? I answer, the general principles of Christianity, in which all these sects were united, and the general principles of English and American liberty, in which all those young men united, and which had united all parties in America in majorities sufficient to assert and maintain her independence.[8]

As late as 1813, John Adams was worried that Jefferson's deism and his so-called "Wall of Separation" did not align with America's origins. This tension becomes evident when we examine the founding documents, which are deeply rooted in Natural Law and Sacred Scripture.

GOD AND THE DECLARATION OF INDEPENDENCE

"Our Constitution was made only for a moral and religious people. It is wholly inadequate to the government of any other."

—John Adams

The Declaration of Independence defends American independence and national sovereignty by a direct appeal to God. The Declaration is a theistic document that unravels without the underpinning of God as the author of nature, law, and providence. It is a rather brief document consisting of 1,458 words, but it invokes God four times in the most crucial sections of the text:

1. "the Laws of Nature and of Nature's God" in the first paragraph.
2. "endowed by their Creator with certain unalienable Rights" in the second paragraph.
3. "appealing to the Supreme Judge of the world" in the final paragraph.
4. "the protection of divine Providence" in the final line of the Declaration.

The opening paragraph justifies the separation of the thirteen colonies from England by appealing to "the Laws of Nature and of Nature's God." This serves as a strong affirmation of the Christian doctrine of Natural Law (which we will discuss below) and the existence of God as its author. It is impossible for an atheist to affirm the Declaration while simultaneously denying the existence of God.

The second paragraph affirms the existence of objective "unalienable Rights" as "endowed by their Creator." The phrase "unalienable rights" refers to rights that are not granted by another. The Latin word *alienus* means "derived from another person," just as *alius* refers to "the identity of another." "Unalienable rights" affirms that human rights are granted not by a king, congress, parliament, or majority consensus. Rights are "unalienable" because they come from God and God alone. An atheist must claim that "rights" are given by a human consensus—not by God. Again, an secular atheist cannot affirm the thesis of the Declaration.

The final paragraph of the Declaration is, in fact, a prayer of supplication that begins by invoking God: "We, therefore, the Representatives of the United States of America, in General Congress, Assembled, appealing to the Supreme Judge of the world." The invocation of "Judge of the World" is explicitly Christian. The language of the Signatories derives from five Bible verses from the

New Testament that directly address Our Lord Jesus Christ as Judge of the World:

1. Because he hath appointed a day wherein he will judge the world in equity, by the man whom he hath appointed; giving faith to all, by raising him up from the dead (Acts 17:31).
2. In the day when God shall judge the secrets of men by Jesus Christ, according to my gospel (Romans 2:16).
3. But thou, why judgest thou thy brother? or thou, why dost thou despise thy brother? For we shall all stand before the judgment seat of Christ (Romans 14:10).
4. For we must all be manifested before the judgment seat of Christ, that everyone may receive the proper things of the body, according as he hath done, whether it be good or evil (2 Corinthians 5:10).
5. I charge thee, before God and Jesus Christ, who shall judge the living and the dead, by his coming, and his kingdom (2 Timothy 4:1).

This final line of the Declaration concludes with the phrase, "with a firm reliance on the protection of divine Providence." This statement resonates with an affirmation found in the biblical book of Wisdom, as printed in the King James Bible under the Apocrypha—a vivid passage that asserts that wicked tyrants may presume to hold dominion over a nation but will ultimately be exiled by "eternal providence":

> For while the wicked thought to be able to have dominion over the holy nation, they themselves being fettered with the bonds of darkness, and a long night, shut up in their houses, lay there exiled from the eternal providence (Wisdom 17:2 KJV).

The Declaration reveals its uniquely Christian foundation. The Founders framed the Constitution in the same way.

DEUTERONOMY AND THE CONSTITUTION

In his groundbreaking study, *The Origins of American Constitutionalism*, political scholar Donald Lutz analyzed the political influences on the American Founders.[9] His research revealed that the Holy Bible was cited more often than any European or Enlightenment thinker. According to Lutz, biblical references constituted about a third of all citations in the works he examined. Among these citations, the book of Deuteronomy emerged as the most frequently referenced text, even surpassing Montesquieu's *The Spirit of Law*. In fact, Deuteronomy was cited nearly twice as often as the writings of John Locke, and the Apostle Paul was mentioned as frequently as Montesquieu and Blackstone, who were among the most-referenced secular scholars.

Why did the Founding Fathers remain so focused on the fifth book of the Bible—Deuteronomy? One reason that Deuteronomy held such prominence in their written discourse is that this biblical book serves as the "Constitution" of the Law of Moses. As the inspired "Constitution of Moses," Deuteronomy details the political and legal framework of Moses for the Israelites, making it particularly relevant to those interested in nation-building. While the New Testament, particularly Paul's teaching in Romans 13, discusses political civility for Christians within the context of the Roman Empire, the book of Deuteronomy provides a detailed blueprint for structuring a nation. The "exodus" of the twelve tribes of Israel (thirteen if you count Levi) out from under the tyranny of Pharaoh nicely parallels the thirteen colonies' "exodus" from the tyranny of King George III. Just as Israel had crossed the Red Sea to escape the

Pharoah, the early Americans were acutely aware that their forebears had also escaped across the sea to this new Promised Land.

The spiritual foundation of the Constitution is supported by John Adams, who famously stated in 1798: "Our Constitution was made only for a moral and religious people. It is wholly inadequate to the government of any other."[10] His statement reflects his belief, as a much younger man in 1756, that the Bible is the best "law book":

> Suppose a nation in some distant Region should take the Bible for their only law Book, and every member should regulate his conduct by the precepts there exhibited! Every member would be obliged in conscience, to temperance, frugality, and industry; to justice, kindness, and charity towards his fellow men; and to piety, love, and reverence toward Almighty God.... What a Eutopia, what a Paradise would this region be.[11]

His conviction is also affirmed in his defense of Christianity in 1796:

> The Christian religion is, above all the religions that ever prevailed or existed in ancient or modern times, the religion of wisdom, virtue, equity, and humanity, let the blackguard Paine say what he will; it is resignation to God, it is goodness itself to man.[12]

If the Declaration of Independence portrays God as both the author of Natural Law and the judge of the world, and the United States Constitution is based on the blueprint of Deuteronomy, how did the United States become infiltrated by a New Secular Religion? The virus was introduced by a misleading interpretation of Thomas Jefferson's "wall of separation between church and state," and that wall has been built wider and higher than any of the founders could have anticipated. We now turn to the Christian theology of government. How does government derive from God, and how have Christians shaped government over the centuries? After establishing this foundation, we will explore twelve strategies for Christian Patriots to transform culture and politics for the greater glory of God.

CHAPTER 4

WHAT IS A CHRISTIAN FORM OF GOVERNMENT?

Before the Christian Patriot pursues a Christian form of government, we must first establish *theologically* what civil government is and who has the right to authorize it. The biblical answer is that God instituted civil government in a twofold manner. First, God established the traditional family as the fundamental unit of human society. Subsequently, God made a covenant with Noah after the flood to authorize municipal rule in line with what we now refer to as civil government.

The Bible establishes the family as God's first human institution. In Genesis 1:27–28, we read, "So God created man in his own image, male and female he created them. And God blessed them, and God said to them, 'Be fruitful and multiply, and fill the earth.'" This command to procreate and steward creation marks the family—man, woman, and children—as the primary unit of human society. The union of Adam and Eve further cemented marriage as the origin of family life: "Therefore a man leaves his father and his mother and cleaves to his wife, and they become one flesh" (Genesis 2:24). C.S. Lewis observed, "The family is the natural unit where affection begins, and from it flows the loyalty that binds communities and nations."[1]

THE COVENANT WITH ADAM

The New Testament also reinforces marriage and the family as the fundamental units of society. The Apostle Paul, in Ephesians 5:25, instructs, "Husbands, love your wives, as Christ loved the church and gave himself up for her." This sacrificial love elevates the family to a reflection of divine unity, a "domestic church." Psalm 126:3 declares, "Behold the inheritance of the Lord are children: the reward, the fruit of the womb." The family, then, is both a gift and a mission, tasked with raising generations in God's image, forming the moral fabric of nations.

In *City of God*, Augustine writes, "The household is the beginning or element of the city, and every beginning is directed to some end of its own kind. Thus, the well-ordered household is the foundation of the well-ordered city" (Book XIX, Chapter 16). For Augustine, the family's harmony—rooted in love and justice—scales upward into the nation. A disordered home, marked by vice or neglect, breeds a disordered society. He ties this to divine order: "The peace of the household is the peace of the city, and the peace of all is the peace of God."

In Augustine's view, the family is the seedbed of virtue, without which nations crumble. Thomas Aquinas adds, "The good of the individual is subordinated to the good of the family, and the good of the family to the good of the community" (*Summa Theologiae* I-II, Q. 90, A. 2). A nation's stability depends on families fulfilling this natural role, as they cultivate citizens capable of civic virtue. Pope Leo XIII, in his 1891 encyclical *Rerum Novarum*, declares, "The family is the origin of human society.... It is the source from which the habits of citizens are formed, and thus the strength or weakness of the state depends upon it."[2] Addressing industrial upheaval, Leo XIII viewed the family as a bulwark against social decay, with its sanctity essential to national well-being.

Pope Pius XI, in *Casti Connubii* (1930), describes marriage as "the principle and foundation of human society," prophetically highlighting that, "the prosperity of the state depends on the peace and unity of the domestic family."[3] He cautions that nations that disregard the sacredness of the family—through divorce or materialism—invite destruction. Pius XI connects this to Genesis, affirming that marriage's divine origin is the basis of societal order. Lutheran thinker Dietrich Bonhoeffer underscored the family's divine purpose: "The family is the cell of the state.... Through its order under God, it shapes the character of a people."[4]

From a Christian perspective, the family is the nucleus of a nation, ordained by God to reflect His love and order. Scripture (Genesis 1:28; Ephesians 5:25) sets forth its divine blueprint—marriage and children as a sacred unity. Augustine and Aquinas describe it as the seed and natural foundation of society, serving as a source of civic virtue and national strength. Protestant leaders like Lewis and Bonhoeffer share this view, regarding the family as the forge of character and a bastion against chaos. A nation flourishes when families flourish, nurturing citizens rooted in faith, love, and justice. As Proverbs 22:6 advises, "Train up a child in the way he should go. And when he is old he will not depart from it." In contrast, a nation that undermines the family—through the policies of the New Secular Religion—sows its own decline. As G.K. Chesterton stated, "The family is itself a wild and living thing; and nothing is so dangerous as to turn the State into a sort of tame thing to crush it.... If we do not keep the family free, we shall not keep anything free."[5]

THE COVENANT WITH NOAH

The covenant with Noah, detailed in Genesis 9, establishes the foundational principles that underlie human government. After the Flood, God's promise to Noah and his descendants provides a universal framework for order, justice, and stewardship, marking the first explicit divine mandate for societal governance. Theologians throughout the centuries see this covenant as the basis of legitimate authority, grounded in God's preservation of creation and humanity's role within it.

In Genesis 9:6, God declares, "Whoever sheds the blood of man, by man shall his blood be shed; for God made man in his own image." This establishes the sanctity of life and the principle of retributive justice, suggesting the need for human authority to enforce laws and penalties. The rainbow sign of the covenant (hijacked by the LGBTQ+ lobby) symbolizes God's commitment to sustaining the world, giving humanity the responsibility to maintain civil order. Unlike the later covenant with Moses at Mount Sinai, the Noahic covenant is universal, applying to all peoples and thus providing a basis for government beyond Israel.

Saint Augustine ties this covenant of God with Noah to the beginning of human governance: "The authority to punish evildoers, as seen in the command against shedding blood, is given to man after the Flood, showing that God entrusts earthly justice to human hands."[6] Augustine views the Noahic covenant as the origin of temporal power, necessary for restraining sin in a fallen world while pointing to divine oversight. Saint Thomas Aquinas confirms the same interpretation of Genesis when he taught, "The precept given to Noah concerning the shedding of blood implies a Natural Law of justice, from which the institution of government derives its right to punish."[7] For Aquinas, the covenant reflects Natural Law—accessible to all humanity—making government a divinely sanctioned necessity to uphold order and protect life, rooted in the imago Dei —image of God.

Protestant theologian Herman Bavinck (1854–1921) connects the Noahic Covenant to the institution of government: "The Noahic covenant, with its laws of life and retribution, lays the groundwork for all human government, as it entrusts mankind with the task of preserving creation under God's promise."[8] Bavinck emphasizes the covenant's stability as the foundation for nations to organize and thrive. James B. Jordan, also a Reformed thinker, adds, "Genesis 9:6 is the charter of government.... It establishes the state's role in wielding the sword, flowing from God's delegation to Noah as mankind's representative."[9] Admittedly, God's covenant with Noah does not provide a detailed constitution. It merely establishes that bloodshed ought to be punished with the death penalty, and it deputizes humans to enforce penalties. A nation's constitution and set of laws are presumably to be derived from Natural Law.

NATURAL LAW AS THE BASIS FOR HUMAN LAW

Natural Law is a philosophical and legal theory found in Genesis but explained in detail by the Apostle Paul in his Epistle to the Romans:

> For when the Gentiles, who have not the law, do by nature those things that are of the law; these having not the law are a law to themselves: who show the work of the law written in their hearts, their conscience bearing witness to them, and their thoughts between themselves accusing, or also defending one another (Romans 2:14–15).

Paul testifies to a "law written in their hearts" in accord with human nature. This Natural Law contains the moral rules inscribed by God in human nature. Since human nature is common to all people, these Natural Laws can be accessed universally by all men.

Saint Thomas Aquinas distilled Natural Law down to the maxim: "good is to be done and pursued, and evil is to be avoided."[10] This first principle leads to the secondary precepts of Natural Law, such as "thou shalt not kill, thou shalt not commit adultery, thou shalt not steal, thou shalt not bear false witness," etc.

Plato, Aristotle, and the Stoic philosophers before Jesus Christ acknowledged the existence of this Natural Law inscribed in the human heart. Roman philosophers who lived nearer to the time of Christ, such as Cicero and Livy, also popularized the belief that a universal Natural Law resided in the heart of man and governed all people if they rationally adhered to it. When Paul wrote his epistle to the Romans, he rightly assumed that his Roman audience also recognized this "law written in their hearts."

The ancient Greek philosophers, the Roman Stoics, and Christians have historically defined all civil human laws as derived from the Natural Law. For Thomas Aquinas, there is a divine, providential "stacking" of law by God in the universe:

1. Eternal Law: The eternal law of God is God's rational order governing creation. It is also called divine providence. It controls the planets, the seasons, and the biological cycles of life.
2. Natural Law: The Natural Law is the participation of human beings in the eternal law of God's providence.[11] This is the "law written in their hearts" according to Romans 2:14. Natural Law pertains to the actions of human persons as moral agents.
3. Human Law: Human law is the practical application of the Natural Law to promote virtue, protect lives and property, enforce justice, and ensure the common good of all.
4. Divine Law: Beyond the human laws of government, which are derived from Natural Law, God further revealed reli-

gious laws and commandments that pertain to those who seek to love God and be saved from sin. Divine Law is essentially the revealed will of God found in the Old and New Testaments. The Sermon on the Mount, the Great Commission, the call to be baptized, and the celebration of the Eucharist are examples that fall under Divine Law.

For Christians, any "civil law" not derived from Natural Law is deemed a false law. A civil law enforcing a one-child policy, mandatory abortion, or genocide does not qualify as a genuine human law because it lacks a foundation in Natural Law. Such false laws do not carry God's authority, lack legal validity, and may be opposed by citizens.[12] Moreover, even obscure laws like "drive no faster than 20 miles per hour in a school zone" qualify as true human laws since they are based on the Natural Law regarding the preservation of human life, especially the lives of children.

Human law, by contrast, is particular and contingent, enacted by rulers or communities to address specific needs. Seeking to preserve lives, one nation may have certain laws regarding harvest and planting that a nation in another geographic region does not enforce. A civil law's legitimacy hinges on its conformity to Natural Law. A law banning theft aligns with the natural inclination to justice; a law mandating idolatry defies reason and God's order, rendering it tyrannical. Daniel and his friends were right to reject Nebuchadnezzar's law to worship a pagan idol.

With these principles in mind, Thomas Aquinas gives the four conditions for a human law to be true and binding for citizens:[13]

1. Ordered to the Common Good: Aquinas argues that the primary purpose of a law is to promote the welfare of the community rather than private interests. He states, "Law is nothing else than an ordinance of reason for the com-

mon good, made by him who has care of the community, and promulgated" (*Summa Theologiae* I-II, Q. 90, A. 4). A just law guides citizens toward mutual flourishing—such as public health regulations—rather than solely benefiting a ruler or an elite group.

2. In accordance with reason and natural law, human law must reflect rational order, deriving from natural law, which in turn mirrors God's eternal law. Aquinas states, "Human law has the nature of law insofar as it partakes of right reason; and it is clear that, in this respect, it is derived from the natural law" (*Summa Theologiae* I-II, Q. 95, A. 2). A law banning theft is rational, upholding justice; one mandating irrational acts (e.g., worshiping a tyrant) lacks legitimacy and becomes violence rather than law. A superfluous law, such as, "You must wear a pink wig every Wednesday," also fails to align with reason.
3. A Law Requires Legitimate Authority: A true law necessitates a proper authority—those entrusted with governance. Aquinas explains, "To order anything to the common good belongs either to the whole people, or to someone who is the vicegerent of the whole people" (*Summa Theologiae* I-II, Q. 90, A. 3). A just law arises from a ruler or body with jurisdiction, such as a legislature, not from a usurper. Without this, it lacks binding force, as authority derives from God's order (Romans 13:1). A private citizen or informal group cannot create rules for others and enforce them without recognized, legitimate authority.
4. Promulgated (made known): For a law to be binding, it must be officially published to those it governs. An unpublished decree isn't a law—citizens cannot obey secret regulations. If a state lowers the speed limit from 80 miles per

hour to 50 miles per hour without publishing it, the police cannot justly issue citations for those driving between 80 and 50 miles per hour. Personal ignorance of the law, by the way, does not invalidate promulgation. If a law is published, a person cannot avoid accountability by claiming personal ignorance; however, it may lessen culpability. Saying "I didn't know hunting bald eagles was illegal" won't excuse you because the decree is properly published to the public. If you engage in hunting, you must know the laws.

Natural Law has been the cornerstone of laws for every Christian civilization, but, sadly, we have lost touch with it. It is well and good to legislate murder as a crime against the teachings of God, Moses, and Jesus Christ. One might also cite biblical verses against homicide. However, one might also appeal to the Natural Law written in the human heart. The inalienable right to life derives from Natural Law and our creation in the image and likeness of God. The protection and sanctity of marriage, as well as of children, also stem from Natural Law. The recognition of private property likewise comes from the Natural Law.

One weakness of contemporary Christian discourse is that Natural Law is often unknown or excluded from public discussion. This may arise from the Protestant belief that all knowledge about God and morality comes from Scripture alone. Nevertheless, Sacred Scripture attests to the existence of Natural Law. Christian Patriots would be wise to recognize and advocate for legislation grounded in Natural Law as a rational and effective strategy. Furthermore, they would gain from enshrining the principle of Natural Law in their constitutions, rights, bills, and courts, as we will explore in a future chapter. After all, the American Declaration of Independence justifies our independence and rights by referencing "the Laws of

Nature" in its opening paragraph. We would not be true Americans if we did not also invoke Natural Law as intended by our Founders. In light of Natural Law, let us consider the prospect of a truly "Christian Constitution."

CHAPTER 5

HISTORY OF CHRISTIAN GOVERNANCE

A nation must have a constitution. A nation must have laws. A nation must have courts. A nation must have leaders. How, then, does a properly ordered nation arise from a collection of families? Philosophers have long debated the foundations of how nations are inaugurated and how they are preserved over time. History provides examples:

1. Monarchy: A powerful "father of fathers" governs the kingdom as king. This form often leads to problems. Is law simply the opinion of one king? Can he be opposed? Can he be removed?
2. Aristocracy or Plutocracy: A council of nobles or aristocrats governs as a parliament or senate. Problems arise with how members of this legislative class are appointed and removed. Are offices inherited? Are they earned? Are they elected? How are they held accountable? Can they be purchased? Do they govern for the common good or for themselves?
3. Democracy: In a direct democracy, rules and decisions are determined by popular vote. Even then, who qualifies to vote in these elections? Are all decisions decided by

common consent of the majority? How are elections kept honest? How is this majority determined? Is the majority always trusted? Who counts the votes? What if the majority votes for sinful laws, such as enslavement, abortion, or unjust wars?

4. Anarchy. Every man for himself. The vulnerable are not protected. The powerful prevail over the weak. How is trade, food, water, and security maintained? Are there trials? Who judges and who enforces?

Notably, the Holy Bible does not provide an explicit blueprint for Christian society. There is no "political Christian constitution" affixed to the final page of the Bible after the Book of Revelation. As we will see, the Founding Fathers of the United States of America searched through the pages of Deuteronomy to discover the best template for establishing a new nation in a new land. However, Deuteronomy is not the only biblical text that has inspired Christians in their pursuit of establishing a Christian nation.

The Old Testament's emphasis on kingship in Jerusalem, Saint Paul's doctrine of regarding the ruler as "God's minister" (Romans 13:4), and the apocalyptic description that "the kings of the earth shall bring their glory and honor" into Heaven (Revelation 21:24) provided the backdrop for supporting Christian kingship for most of Christian history.

Before the birth of Jesus Christ, Greek philosophers like Socrates, Plato, and Aristotle grappled with the conventional forms of government. In Book 8 of the *Republic*, Socrates outlines the best and worst forms of government as follows:

1. Aristocracy (rule by wise philosopher-kings): The best government, based on virtue and reason for the common good.
2. Timocracy (rule by honor-driven warriors): A government driven by military values and the virtue of fortitude.

3. Oligarchy (rule by the wealthy few): A government focused on wealth and property, ruled by those who have a financial stake.
4. Democracy (rule by the people): A government of majority rule, prone to disorder and instability.
5. Tyranny (rule by a tyrant): The worst, as it is based on selfishness, injustice, and oppression of the people by a single tyrant who enshrines his will as law.

The histories of most ancient peoples reveal a cycle of monarchical rule characterized by Aristocracy (wise kings) and Tyranny (selfish kings). Even the Old Testament chronicles the rise and fall of good and bad kings over Israel and Judah. Rarely do powerful nations see governance by a Senate—the notable exception being the Roman Republic, which lasted 482 years, from its traditional founding in 509 BC to its transition into the Roman Empire in 27 BC under the Caesars. For the first three centuries of Christianity, Christians endured persistent persecution by Roman emperors. They knew only tyranny.

When a significant number of Christians began acquiring political offices in Armenia (starting in AD 301) and Rome (beginning in AD 313), they started transforming the inherited pagan structures of government and conceiving ways to align their kingdoms with Christ's kingdom in Heaven. The earliest Christians viewed this as prophesied in the book of Daniel, where the four successive pagan kingdoms of Babylon, Medo-Persia, Greece, and Rome are ultimately handed over to Christians:

> These four great beasts are four kingdoms, which shall arise out of the earth. But the saints of the most high God shall take the kingdom: and they shall possess the kingdom for ever and ever (Daniel 7:17–18).

The Book of Revelation also revealed how the pagan Beast and the Whore of Babylon would be overcome, and it demonstrated how the anti-Christian kingdoms would come to be handed over to Christians. For Christians in the first three centuries, this vision was more apocalyptic and centered on the end times. However, with the conversion of King Tiridates III of Armenia in AD 301 and the Roman Emperor Constantine's Edict of Milan in AD 313, the actual conversion of pagan kingdoms to Christ became a reality. The prophecy of Daniel was unfolding in real time: "But the saints of the most high God shall take the kingdom [of the beasts]" (Daniel 7:17).[1]

From 301 forward, the pagan nations fell like successive dominoes to Christianity and Christian rule. The list below illustrates the progressive adoption of Christianity by nations:

301: Armenia

313: Roman Edict of Milan

319: Christianization Georgia

325: Kingdom of Aksum/Ethiopia

337: Roman Empire (baptism of Constantine I)

411: Kingdom of Burgundy

496: Franks

c. 558: Christianization of Ireland

c. 563: Picts

589: Visigoths

591: Lombards

601–604: Kent, East Anglia, and Essex

c. 620: Alemanni

627: Northumbria); East Anglia returns from Chalcedonian to pagan

630: East Anglia returns from pagan

635: Wessex

653: Lombards

653: Essex

655: Mercia

675: Sussex

696: Bavaria

724: Thuringia

734: Frisians

785: Saxons

840s: Navarre

863: Moravia

864: Christianization of Bulgaria

c. 869: Christianization of the Serbs

879: Croatia

884: Bohemia

911: Normans

960: Denmark

966: Christianization of Poland

c. 989: Christianization of Kievan Rus'

995: Norway

999: Faroe Islands

1000 Christianization of Hungary and the first real Christian king

1000: Christianization of Iceland

1007: Keraites of Mongolia

1008: Sweden

1054: Byzantine Empire, Kingdom of Georgia, Bulgaria, Serbs, and Rus' become Orthodox Catholic with East-West Schism while Western Europe becomes Roman Catholic

c. 1200: (Southwestern) Finland

1387: Christianization of Lithuania

The conversion of nations to Christianity continued decade after decade and century after century, spreading from the Mediterranean regions outward to the Americas, Africa, Asia, and Australia. The United States of America was not especially unique in its appeal to Natural Law and biblical passages. Christian Roman historians depicted Constantine as a "new Moses," who defeated the "Pharaoh" Maximinus at the water crossing of the Roman Milvian Bridge, having "let my people go" from the savage Roman persecution of Christians.[2] It was common for most Christian empires, kingdoms, and nations to reframe their leaders as a New Moses or New David.

Beginning in Armenia and the Roman Empire, Christians began to hold public office and abolish pagan laws, rites, and customs. Initially, these changes were gradual and somewhat subtle, including the ban on crucifixion and the end of gladiatorial games. By AD 429, the Christian Roman Emperor Theodosius II announced his intention for the Roman Senate to form a committee to codify all Christian laws in effect from Constantine's reign to his own time. Twenty-two scholars, divided into two teams, worked for nine years, starting in AD 429, to compile what would become the *Theodosian Code*. The chief scholarly overseer of this work was Antiochus Chuzon, who directed a collection of sixteen books containing over 2,500 constitutions. It marked the first formulation of Roman law since the ancient Roman Twelve Tables—but this time, it was Christian.

CHRISTIAN DARK AGES?

The initial establishment of Christian laws and governance was far from perfect. However, the transition of numerous pagan kingdoms to Christian ones was nothing short of miraculous. Unfortunately, Enlightenment philosophers and historians—who were generally atheistic or, at best, nonreligious—labeled this era as the "Dark Ages," contrasting it with their own "Enlightenment," which represented a secular break from Europe's Christian past.

Thinkers like René Descartes (1596–1650), Baruch Spinoza (1632–1677), John Locke (1632–1704), and Voltaire (1694–1778) redefined philosophy and politics through humanism, separating it from its traditional Christian consensus. While Enlightenment thinkers came from Jewish, Protestant, and Catholic backgrounds, their dismissal of the so-called "dark ages" relied on the post-Reformation belief that the twelve Christian centuries between Constantine and Luther were characterized by "darkness." The concept of the "dark ages" is summarized by theologian Theodore Beza (1519–1605) who quipped in Latin, *post tenebras lux*—"after the darkness is light." Sadly, the brightness of Christian influence began to dim across Europe beginning in the seventeenth and eighteenth centuries.

The term "Dark Ages" evokes images of cultural stagnation, ignorance, and decline. However, this perspective—rooted in Enlightenment thinking and popularized by later secular historians—fails to account for the significant achievements that occurred during the Middle Ages. Far from being a dark and regressive time, the Middle Ages laid the foundation for much of Western civilization. Christianity, in particular, was a driving force for intellectual accounts of social and cultural development, fostering advancements in education, science, philosophy, art, and governance. Far from being an age of darkness, the Midde Ages were a vital period of transformation that set the stage for the Renaissance and the modern world.

While figures of the Enlightenment like Voltaire and Gibbon sought to disparage Christian civilizations as "dark," modern historians have increasingly debunked the notion of a regressive "Dark Age" between AD 500 and AD 1500. Rather than being a wasteland of ignorance, the Middle Ages saw the slow but steady rebuilding of Christian civilization. Modern historians often celebrate the remarkable era of the ancient Roman Empire, which lasted for 503 years. Yet, for most of that time, the ancient Roman Empire was plagued by tyranny, persecution, slavery, and oppression. In contrast, the Christian Holy Roman Empire lasted a much more impressive 844 years. While not perfect, the Holy Roman Empire fostered saints, missionaries, universities, literature, history, wider literacy, theologians, poets, sainted rulers, and a network of monasteries and schools as centers of learning. Most people today do not fully appreciate how the Holy Roman Empire outperformed the ancient Roman Empire.

THE CHURCH AS A BEACON OF CIVILIZATION

Central to the transformation of the Roman Empire was the Church. Since the first century, Christians have identified the prophecies of the prophet Daniel as a foreshadowing of the gradual transformation of the fourth and final pagan kingdom into the Kingdom of God. Daniel outlined four symbolic kingdoms and foretold that during the fourth kingdom, the Messianic Son of God would be born and change these pagan kingdoms into the Kingdom of God. He provided this prophecy twice: once in Daniel 2 and again in Daniel 7, as shown in the table below:

Daniel 2 Vision	**Daniel 7 Vision**	**Christian Fulfillment**
Dream of 4-Fold Idol	Dream of 4 Beasts	4 Pagan Empires
1) Head of Gold 2) Chest of Silver 3) Legs of Bronze 4) Feet of Clay and Iron 5) Destroyed by Stone	1) Lion 2) Bear 3) Leopard 4) Horned Beast 5) Destroyed by Son of Man	1) Babylonians 2) Medo-Persians 3) Greeks 4) Romans 5) Conquered by Son of Man on Roman Cross
Daniel 2:44–45: "But in the days of those kingdoms the God of heaven will set up a kingdom that shall never be destroyed, and his kingdom shall not be delivered up to another people, and it shall break in pieces, and shall consume all these kingdoms, and itself shall stand for ever. According as thou sawest that the stone was cut out of the mountain without hands, and broke in pieces, the clay, and the iron, and the brass, and the silver, and the gold, the great God hath shewn the king what shall come to pass hereafter, and the dream is true, and the interpretation thereof is faithful."	Daniel 7:23–27: "The fourth beast shall be the fourth kingdom upon earth, which shall be greater than all the kingdoms, and shall devour the whole earth, and shall tread it down, and break it in pieces.... And that the kingdom, and power, and the greatness of the kingdom, under the whole heaven, may be given to the people of the saints of the most High: whose kingdom is an everlasting kingdom, and all kings shall serve him, and shall obey him."	Revelation 19:16–20: "And he hath on his garment, and on his thigh written: KING OF KINGS, AND LORD OF LORDS.... And the beast was taken, and with him the false prophet, who wrought signs before him, wherewith he seduced them who received the character of the beast, and who adored his image. These two were cast alive into the pool of fire, burning with brimstone."

Christ was born under the census of the Roman Emperor Augustus "in the fullness of time," spent his entire life within the Roman Empire (Judea and Egypt were Roman provinces). He was "crucified under Pontius Pilate" and killed on a Roman cross. Jesus Christ is the "Stone" that the builders rejected in Daniel 2 and the "Son of Man" who conquers the fourth kingdom (Rome) to bring about a "kingdom without end."

Starting in the fifth century, the Church filled the void by preserving classical learning and providing a unifying cultural and moral framework for Europe, rooted in a distinct Christian formation. This is why Enlightenment atheists and philosophers termed the era as "dark," when, in fact, Christendom was emerging. Thousands of copies of the Bible were meticulously hand copied and distributed throughout the world by monks who worked tirelessly with quill and ink under lamplight. Rather than being confined to a few select libraries in Rome and Alexandria, classical texts were copied, disseminated, and preserved across all nations. This included not just Scripture but also classical works of medicine, philosophy, history, and science. Without these efforts, much of the ancient world's intellectual heritage would have been lost. From AD 500 to 1000, there were an estimated 500 to 1,000 monasteries and libraries in Europe, and, over time, that number grew to 3,000 monasteries.

Monasteries were not merely repositories of knowledge; they also served as centers of technological innovation and economic growth. The Benedictine Rule, composed around AD 516, emphasized labor, learning, and prayer, fostering a balanced life that encouraged both spiritual and intellectual pursuits. They introduced new agricultural practices, such as crop rotation and enhanced plowing techniques, which increased food production and supported population growth. Monastic communities also played a vital role in promoting literacy, education, medical care, orphanages, universities, travel hostels, and social welfare.

THE PROLIFERATION OF THE HOLY BIBLE

Perhaps one of the greatest misconceptions of the medieval era was that there was a strict restriction on the Holy Bible. From the time of the Apostles until the 4th century, manuscripts of the Bible were often partial or incomplete. The amount of labor, skill, and scholarship required to produce a Bible by hand prevented most people—and even many churches—from owning a complete collection of the Sacred Scriptures. The proliferation of the Holy Bible began with the Roman Emperor Constantine's order for published Bibles, which he formally decreed around AD 325.

The Roman Emperor Constantine commissioned and funded the production of fifty hand-copied editions of the Holy Bible. These copies were meant to be deluxe, parchment-bound codices (books bound with a spine) intended for use by the churches in the imperial city of Constantinople. This order is noted in historical records, especially by the 4th-century church historian Eusebius of Caesarea, who documented Constantine's desire to ensure that churches in the East would possess accurate, high-quality copies of the Bible.

According to Eusebius, Constantine ordered the copies to be made in Greek, and he requested that they be based on the correct texts. Eusebius himself was tasked with overseeing the production of these fifty copies. He mentions the Bible project in his *Life of Constantine*, in which he explains that Constantine was particularly interested in promoting unity and providing the Church with official and authoritative texts. These Bibles were significant because they were produced using parchment, which was more durable than papyrus, and were bound in a way that made them easier to read than the rolled scrolls that had been used before.

The two oldest manuscripts of the Bible are thought to have originated from this era, but may not belong to that original order of fifty Bibles. *Codex Sinaiticus* is one of the earliest and most complete surviving manuscripts of the Bible in Greek. It dates from the 4th century, and while it is not directly linked to Constantine's commission, it is believed to have been produced around this time. Another significant 4th-century Greek manuscript, *Codex Vaticanus*, is also considered to be from this period and may possibly belong to the production of Bibles during Constantine's reign.

About sixty years later, in AD 382, Pope Damasus in Rome commissioned the linguist Saint Jerome to translate the entire Bible into Latin—the most commonly spoken language of the Western Roman Empire. This official Latin translation is known as the "Sacra Biblia Vulgata" or "Holy Bible in the Vulgar Language," as it was not in the original Greek. The Latin Bible was completed around AD 405 and became the standard Bible in the West.

Many Christians have been misled to believe that greedy monks and bishops wanted to keep the Bible hidden from public view, and that vernacular translations of Sacred Scripture appeared only after John Wycliffe (1395) or Martin Luther (1534). This is a broad statement that fails to accurately reflect the eleven centuries from 300 to 1400. Additionally, the clergy read at least thirty verses from the Bible daily to the laity during church services. Historians are also uncovering more manuscripts that indicate the existence of vernacular Bibles long before Wycliffe. Numerous vernacular translations were created over the centuries before 1500:

1. The Old English Translation of Bede
    a) The Venerable Bede himself did not complete a full Bible translation into Old English, but he did translate portions of the Bible into Old English sometime before AD 730. His work mainly involved translating the Gospel of John into the vernacular Old English for use in Anglo-Saxon England.

2. The Old English Heptateuch (AD 700s)

   b) Details: The earliest known translation of parts of the Bible into Old English was the Heptateuch, which included the first seven books of the Bible. It was translated from the Latin Vulgate and was most likely intended for Anglo-Saxon laymen and clergy.

3. The Old Church Slavonic Bible (AD 880)

   c) The first translation of the Bible into a Slavic language. Cyril and Methodius, two Byzantine missionary monks, created the Glagolitic alphabet, which was later replaced by the Cyrillic alphabet. They translated portions of the Bible, including the Gospels, for the Slavic peoples of the Balkans.

4. The Wessex Gospels (ca. 10th century):

   d) The Wessex Gospels are the first known complete translation of the Gospels (Matthew, Mark, Luke, and John) into Old English. These translations were likely commissioned by King Alfred the Great (ca. 849–899 AD) in the late 9th century as part of his larger effort to educate the Anglo-Saxon population and promote Bible reading. The Wessex Gospels are also known as the "King Alfred Gospels." King Alfred is often associated with efforts to translate important Christian texts into the vernacular for broader accessibility.

5. The Dutch Bible (ca. 12th century)

   e) The early translations of the Bible into Dutch were based on the Latin Vulgate and included the Gospels and other portions of the Bible. These translations were important for the Dutch-speaking regions of medieval Europe, particularly in areas like the Low Countries.

6. The French Bible (ca. 1200)

    f) This translation was not a complete Bible but rather a fragmented translation of the Scriptures into Old French. It was based on the Latin Vulgate and was primarily used by the clergy and noble classes in France.

7. The Castilian Bible (Alfonsine Bible, ca. 1280)

    g) Known as the Alfonsine Bible, this was the first full translation of the Bible into Castilian Spanish. King Alfonso X commissioned the work for his Spanish-speaking population.

8. The German Bible (Early German translations) (ca. 1466–1470)

    h) Translated sometime before 1470, this is the first vernacular German Bible. It provided accessibility to the Holy Bible for the German-speaking populations of central Europe, decades before Martin Luther created his translation. In fact, recent scholarship reveals that Martin Luther knew of these German translations and often drew from them for his own version.

9. The Italian Bible (ca. 1471)

    i) The first full Italian Bible translation was produced by the Augustinian monk Niccolò Malermi in the late 15th century. This marked the beginning of translating the Bible into the Italian vernacular, helping to spread biblical knowledge among the Italian-speaking populace.

UNIVERSITIES AND LITERARY ACHIEVEMENTS

One of the most significant contributions of Christianity to civilization was the establishment of the university system. The earliest universities—such as those in Bologna, Paris, and Oxford—were founded in the 11th and 12th centuries with the support of the Church. These institutions became the intellectual centers of Europe, where scholars debated theology, philosophy, law, medicine, and the natural sciences.

The medieval university system established the foundation for modern education. During this period, previously unknown works of Plato and Aristotle were rediscovered and integrated into Christian philosophy largely due to scholars like Thomas Aquinas, who blended classical thought with Christian theology. This intellectual movement, called Scholasticism, emphasized reason, logic, and systematic inquiry, challenging the idea that the Middle Ages were a time of unthinking dogmatism. In fact, many scientific advancements took place during this time. Medieval scholars made significant contributions to fields such as astronomy, mathematics, medicine, and mechanics. The so-called "Scientific Revolution" of the early modern period did not emerge from nowhere; it was built on centuries of medieval scholarship.

One example is Boethius, a Christian politician and scholar who translated and preserved the works of Aristotle and other Greek philosophers. Sometime around AD 500, Boethius wrote *On the Division of Nature*, addressing the structure of the natural world and how it can be understood rationally. Although it is more focused on logic and metaphysics, it also touches on the organization of the physical universe, which influenced later scholastic thought.

John Philoponus, a significant Christian philosopher and scholar in Alexandria, questioned certain aspects of Aristotelian cosmology and natural philosophy while also incorporating Christian theology. His works on natural philosophy, including *Physica* (Natural Philosophy) and *De Caelo et Mundo* (On the Heavens and the Earth), sought to clarify natural phenomena in the context of Christian thought.

Gregory of Tours (AD 538–594) was a bishop and historian, and while his writings were more focused on church history and theological matters, he also explored aspects of natural phenomena in his writings. He included descriptions of miracles and supernatural events, which often reflected how medieval Christians understood the natural world and divine intervention.

Gregory the Great (d. 604) emphasized the practical application of Christian doctrine in everyday life, especially regarding pastoral care, salvation, and the church's role in the world. In his work *Moral Exegesis of Job,* he interpreted the Book of Job as a commentary that combines biblical exegesis with practical moral teaching. Gregory highlighted that suffering in life has a redemptive purpose, and his approach to interpreting Scripture for moral guidance greatly influenced later Christian thought. His significant and historical work *Dialogues* primarily centered on the lives of Italian holy men and women and the miracles attributed to them, particularly St. Benedict.

Isidore of Seville (ca. AD 560–636) was a prominent Christian scholar, theologian, and bishop in Seville, Spain. His extensive writings had a profound impact on medieval scholarship and the preservation of classical knowledge. Isidore's *De Natura Rerum* (On the

Nature of Things) attempted to explain the natural world from a theological perspective. In this work, Isidore wrote about the cosmos, elements, seasons, and various natural phenomena, combining biblical creation narratives with classical philosophy. His *History of the Kings of the Goths, Vandals, and Suevi* documented the history of the Visigoths, Vandals, and Suevi, the Germanic tribes that had settled in Spain and parts of the Western Roman Empire. Isidore's *Sententiarum* (Sentences) organized theological maxims or opinions on various subjects such as doctrine, ethics, and Christian sanctification. This text served as a foundation for later theological works, offering a summary of Christian doctrine that was accessible to theologians and scholars. Isidore of Seville's *De Anima* (On the Soul) is a theological and philosophical text that addressed the nature of the human soul and the relationship between the body and the soul. While it's more concerned with theology than scientific analysis, it provides valuable insights into medieval thought on human psychology, physiology, and spirituality.

The Anglo-Saxon monk Venerable Bede (ca. AD 672–735), in his *On the Nature of Things*, mentioned that the Earth is round and how this was an accepted belief in both Christian and classical scholarship in his time. His most significant contribution to Christian scholarship is his historical writings. His most famous work, *The Ecclesiastical History of the English People*, remains one of the foundational texts for understanding the history of Christianity in England and the spread of Christianity in Anglo-Saxon Britain. The work chronicles the history of the Christian Church in Britain, from the Roman period through the 7th century, and it is especially valuable for its detailed accounts of the missions of Saint Augustine of Canterbury and the conversion of the Anglo-Saxons to Christianity.

Literary classics in vernacular languages were produced during this time, such as *Beowulf* (ca. 8th–11th century), the epic Old English poem about a hero who battles monsters and a dragon in a haunting Nordic setting. The *Song of Roland* (ca. 11th century) is a French epic poem based on the Battle of Roncesvalles, showcasing themes of chivalry and heroism. The *Poem of the Cid* (ca. 1207) is a Spanish epic poem about Rodrigo Díaz de Vivar, the Cid, and his role in Spain's Reconquista. The *Divine Comedy* by Dante Alighieri (1320) is an Italian epic poem detailing the journey of the landscape of Hell, Purgatory, and finally Paradise. *The Canterbury Tales* by Geoffrey Chaucer (1387–1400) is an episodic collection of stories told by pilgrims on their devotional pilgrimage to visit the tomb of Saint Thomas Becket in Canterbury. Its lampooning satire reveals a high intellect and a blend of pious faith with cynicism about political and religious abuses of the time.

ART, ARCHITECTURE, AND CULTURE

The so-called "Dark Ages" produced an enduring legacy in art and architecture that continues to impress pilgrims and tourists centuries after their creation. Rather than being a cultural void, the Christian Middle Ages yielded some of the most magnificent works of art and architecture in human history. Romanesque and Gothic cathedrals, with their soaring spires, intricate stained-glass windows, and awe-inspiring sculptures, stand as testaments to the creativity and ingenuity of medieval artisans. These structures were not merely places of worship; they served as symbols of a unified cultural and spiritual vision.

Medieval art, often dismissed as simplistic compared with later Renaissance works, was deeply symbolic and richly layered with meaning. Illuminated manuscripts, mosaics, and religious paintings conveyed complex theological ideas in visually striking ways. Music, too, flourished during the Middle Ages, with the development of Gregorian chant and early forms of polyphony that would later evolve into the rich musical traditions of the Renaissance.

THE BRIGHT LEGACY OF THE "DARK AGES"

The so-called "Dark Ages" were anything but dark. This period saw the preservation and transformation of classical knowledge, the rise of universities, significant scientific and technological advances, and the flowering of art and architecture. At the heart of this transformation was the Christian Church, which not only preserved the intellectual heritage of the ancient world but also created new institutions and ideas that would shape the future of Western civilization.

Rather than being a time of regression, the Middle Ages were a period of resilience, adaptation, and innovation. The legacy of this era is all around us—in our legal systems, educational institutions, artistic traditions, and moral values. To dismiss the Middle Ages as a dark and backward time is to overlook the profound contributions it made to the development of the modern world. Indeed, it was in the so-called "Dark Ages" that the seeds of Western civilization were sown, nurtured by the light of Christian faith and the tireless efforts of countless scholars, artists, and thinkers.

THE BIBLE AND CHRISTIAN LAW

The foundation of the Theodosian Code and the constitutions and laws of subsequent Christian nations (including the United States of America) came from two sources for law, order, and justice. The first source is Natural Law, which we have covered above. The second source is divine revelation, which was received over time as Apostolic Tradition and Sacred Scripture: "Brethren, stand fast and hold the traditions which you have learned, whether by word or by our epistle" (2 Thessalonians 2:14). For those insisting on Scripture alone, the official list of canonical books in the Holy Bible would not be officially canonized and distributed as "the Bible" for centuries after the resurrection. As the Apostle Paul indicates, some form of tradition would have sustained the earliest Christians.

Natural Law holds the first place in government. The second source is Sacred Scripture—the Holy Bible. In our secular environment, we might feel uncomfortable quoting our Bible as God's truth and "imposing" our religion on others. We may also fear that we might be mocked and ridiculed for quoting Sacred Scripture in public discourse. What is the source of this fear? Do we doubt the truth of God's word? Is it true only for us, or is it objectively true for the whole world?

Consider the fact that the New Secular Religion quotes their slogans and studies without hesitation. Why is it permissible for radical Leftists and Liberals to quote their "prophets" but not permissible for Christians to quote the Word of God? Why is it permissible for politicians to quote Malcolm X, Karl Marx, Mahatma Gandhi, Barack Obama, Che Guevara, Gloria Steinem, and Margaret Sanger, but forbidden for Christian politicians to quote Moses, David, Isaiah, Jeremiah, Daniel, Peter, Paul, and John? Moreover, if the Declaration of Independence and the US Constitution are based on the teachings of Christ (as affirmed by John Adams), why can't we quote the Lord Jesus Christ in political discourse?

The Muslim in Arabia (or in London) does not shy away from citing Muhammad. The Hindu in India does not hesitate to quote the Vedas. The atheist in Europe does not recoil from citing Nietzsche. Yet it is the unfortunate Christian, pounded with the concept of "separation of church and state," who fears referencing Jesus Christ while existing in a Christian nation that is being taken away from him.

The New Secular Religion currently demands our acceptance of fifty to seventy different "genders," citing "experts" and journal articles. It imposes this view on schools, libraries, universities, and corporations. Individuals may lose their jobs, be canceled, or denied access if they disagree. Meanwhile, pitiful Christians stand by and say, "But I don't want to impose my religion on others." Christians are perfectly justified in quoting Jesus Christ, the foundation of our society, who taught: "But from the beginning of the creation, God made them male and female" (Mark 10:6).

The New Secular Religion currently demands unrestricted access to abortion. They advocate for terminating pregnancies up to nine months or during delivery and even oppose the Born Alive Act, which requires medical care for infants who survive abortion and are born alive. They claim, "It's just a clump of cells." The Christian must respond with confidence: "For you created my inmost being; you knit me together in my mother's womb. I praise you because I am fearfully and wonderfully made" (Psalm 138:13–16). And they must reaffirm this stance: "The Lord hath called me from the womb; from the womb of my mother hath he been mindful of my name" (Isaiah 49:1).

Why are we afraid to quote from the Bible if it serves as our foundation, origin, and bedrock? Even if one were to accept the most radical doctrine of "separation of church and state," nothing prohibits a governor, congressman, senator, judge, or president from citing Moses, David, Jesus, or the Apostles to justify laws or policies. A Christian should have confidence that his God, faith, Scripture, and the inherited Christian legacy of the West are true, and he must uphold that truth in the public square. If he shrinks back, a vacuum is created, and Satan and his New Secular Religion will fill it, imposing *their beliefs* upon us and our children. Having established the Christian origin of America, our foundation of Natural Law and Sacred Scripture, and the obligation to publicly retain our Christian beliefs and morality in the political sphere, let us now examine twelve ways we can create one nation under God.

STRATEGY 1

CHRIST IN THE SOUL

"But this shall be the covenant that I will make with the house of Israel, after those days, saith the Lord: I will give my law in their hearts, and I will write it in their minds: and I will be their God, and they shall be my people" (Jeremiah 31:33).

The first and highest goal of the Christian Patriot is inward conversion by faith in Jesus Christ, and then subsequently an overflow of joy in sharing the good news with others. The transformation of culture and politics begins in *our* hearts. Jeremiah the prophet foretold that the new covenant and new law will be written in our minds and hearts. No amount of external legislation will make us righteous before God. No amount of external legislation will make a nation godly. The goodness of the nation depends on the goodness of the people.

We could have a constitution recognizing the Holy Trinity, acknowledging Christ as resurrected, allowing Christian prayer in schools, and having the Ten Commandments engraved in every courthouse—but if the people hate God, the nation will be lawless. A perfect example of this is ancient Israel. They were the only divinely instituted civil government in history. Their constitution was inspired by God and penned by none other than Moses. They received laws directly from God. God chose David as king and appointed his successors as monarchs. The temple and priesthood received both divine and political sanction. Prophets arose in every age to teach the people. And yet, time and again, the people of Israel rebelled against God and broke His laws.

- The Lord said to Moses: "See that this people is stiff necked" (Exodus 32:9).
- "Woe to the sinful nation, a people laden with iniquity, a wicked seed, ungracious children: they have forsaken the Lord, they have blasphemed the Holy One of Israel, they are gone away backwards" (Isaiah 1:4).
- "But the heart of this people is become hard of belief and provoking, they are revolted and gone away" (Jeremiah 5:23).
- "You stiff necked and uncircumcised in heart and ears, you always resist the Holy Spirit: as your fathers did, so do you also" (Acts 7:51).

Ancient Israel had divine laws and an infallible constitution. Nevertheless, they had rebellious hearts and frequently rejected their gods in favor of idols. This is why we needed a New Covenant that transformed us internally—the law of God living in our hearts. One might say that the new law is the indwelling of the Holy Spirit within us.

Our Lord Jesus Christ taught that salvation and inner transformation come from a genuine faith, which is rooted first in love for God and then in love for our neighbors. In his Sermon on the Mount, Christ stated, "Seek ye therefore first the kingdom of God, and his justice, and all these things shall be added unto you" (Matthew 6:33). The sequence of action for the Christian Patriot is first to evangelize ourselves, then our families, and finally our culture and nation.

EVANGELIZE YOUR HEART

English speakers have inherited, by no fault of their own, a linguistic confusion about the "gospel" and "evangelism." In the original Greek New Testament, the word for gospel is *euangelion* and the word for evangelism is *euangelismos*. Even if you are not a Greek scholar, you can perceive that the Greek words are alike. *Euangelion* is a composite Greek word:

eu meaning good
angelos meaning messenger or message

You likely already know that an *angel* of God is a messenger of God. Our term angel derives from this same Greek word. Thus, the *euangelion* is simply the "good message" or "good news." When this Greek word *euangelion* was translated into Old English in the 7th–8th century, it was translated as "godspel:"

gōd meaning good
spel meaning news or message

Modern English receives godspel as "gospel." The books of Matthew, Mark, Luke, and John are called the four Gospels because they record the good news of Jesus Christ. Strictly speaking, the gospel is the good news. The process of proclaiming that good news is *euangelismos* or "evangelism." We might hold connotations about this word by associating the word "televangelists" or reduce it to a denomination of Christians who are "evangelicals." However, the very center of the teachings of Jesus Christ and the New Testament is the *euangelion* or "gospel."

WHAT IS THE GOSPEL?

The first mention of the gospel in the New Testament occurs in Matthew: "Jesus went about all Galilee, teaching in their synagogues, and preaching the gospel of the kingdom: and healing all manner of sickness and every infirmity, among the people" (Matthew 4:23). Mark opens his Gospel: "The beginning of the gospel of Jesus Christ, the Son of God" (Mark 1:1). The Gospel is a specific message of Good News that must be received by repentance and faith in Jesus Christ as Lord, Savior, and Son of God.

This message is a narrative that requires the consent of belief. In the Acts of the Apostles, Saint Peter preaches the Good News beginning at Pentecost: "Peter standing up with the eleven, lifted up his voice, and spoke to them: Ye men of Judea, and all you that dwell in Jerusalem, be this known to you, and with your ears receive my words" (Acts 2:14). Peter then proclaims that Jesus Christ was crucified, died, buried, and then raised from the dead:

Acts 2:22–36

22 "Ye men of Israel, hear these words: Jesus of Nazareth, a man approved of God among you, by miracles, and wonders, and signs, which God did by him, in the midst of you, as you also know:

23 This same being delivered up, by the determinate counsel and foreknowledge of God, you by the hands of wicked men have crucified and slain.

24 Whom God hath raised up, having loosed the sorrows of hell, as it was impossible that he should be holden by it.

25 For David saith concerning him: I foresaw the Lord before my face: because he is at my right hand, that I may not be moved.

26 For this my heart hath been glad, and my tongue hath rejoiced: moreover my flesh also shall rest in hope.

27 Because thou wilt not leave my soul in hell, nor suffer thy Holy One to see corruption.

28 Thou hast made known to me the ways of life: thou shalt make me full of joy with thy countenance.

29 Ye men, brethren, let me freely speak to you of the patriarch David; that he died, and was buried; and his tomb is with us to this present day.

30 Whereas therefore he was a prophet, and knew that God hath sworn to him with an oath, that of the fruit of his loins one should sit upon his throne.

31 Foreseeing this, he spoke of the resurrection of Christ. For neither was he left in hell, neither did his flesh see corruption.

32 This Jesus hath God raised again, whereof all we are witnesses.

33 Being exalted therefore by the right hand of God, and having received of the Father the promise of the Holy Ghost, he hath poured forth this which you see and hear.

34 For David ascended not into heaven; but he himself said: The Lord said to my Lord, sit thou on my right hand,

35 Until I make thy enemies thy footstool.

36 Therefore let all the house of Israel know most certainly, that God hath made both Lord and Christ, this same Jesus, whom you have crucified."

The preaching of Saint Peter called for an active decision on the part of his Jewish listeners.

Acts 2:37–39

37 "Now when they [the Jews] had heard these things, they had compunction in their heart, and said to Peter, and to the rest of the apostles: What shall we do, men and brethren?

38 But Peter said to them: Repent and be baptized every one of you in the name of Jesus Christ, for the remission of your sins: and you shall receive the gift of the Holy Spirit.

39 For the promise is to you, and to your children, and to all that are far off, whomsoever the Lord our God shall call."

The message above preached by the Apostle Peter is strictly the *euangelion* or gospel. We must accept it as true and conform our lives to it, or we must reject it. There is no middle way.

By the second century, Christians identified other true Christians by the profession of a *symbolon*—the Greek word for "pushing together." Historically, a symbolon could be two halves of a broken bone or two halves of a broken piece of pottery that each party kept. When they were brought together and accurately fit together, an identity was re-ratified. Thus, a symbolon is any pledge, token, ticket, certificate, or sign used for identification. Nowadays, we may think of it as a password, face recognition, or fingerprint verification.

In the 200s, the bishops Saint Cyprian and Saint Firmilian spoke of a symbolon as verification used by Christians to recognize one another. It was a memorized creed or profession of orthodox faith. Saint Ambrose wrote about an official *Symbolum Apostolicum* or "Apostolic Creed" confessed by all true Christians at their baptism and throughout their lives.

Second-century Christians such as Tertullian and Irenaeus cite the "Apostolic Symbolon," or Apostolic Creed, in their writings. In essence, it was the verbal profession of faith that a person had to profess publicly before receiving Trinitarian water baptism. It has come down to us as the "Apostles' Creed," and tradition proposes that each of Christ's twelve Apostles contributed the *twelve* doctrinal affirmations in the Apostles' Creed:

Apostles' Creed	**Author of each stanza**
1. I believe in God, the Father almighty, creator of heaven and earth.	1. Peter
2. I believe in Jesus Christ,	2. John
3. his only Son, our Lord,	3. James son of Zebedee

Apostles' Creed

1. I believe in God, the Father almighty, creator of heaven and earth.
2. I believe in Jesus Christ, his only Son, our Lord,
3. who was conceived by the Holy Spirit and born of the Virgin Mary.
4. He suffered under Pontius Pilate, was crucified, died, and was buried,
5. He descended to hell.
6. The third day he rose again from the dead.
7. He ascended into heaven and is seated at the right hand of God the Father almighty.
8. From thence He shall come to judge the living and the dead.
9. I believe in the Holy Spirit,
10. the holy Catholic Church, the communion of saints,
11. the forgiveness of sins,
12. the resurrection of the body, and the life everlasting. Amen.

Author of each stanza

1. Peter
2. John
3. James son of Zebedee
4. Andrew
5. Philip
6. Thomas
7. Bartholomew
8. Matthew
9. James son of Alphaeus
10. Simon the Zealot
11. Jude Thaddaeus
12. Matthias

The above text of the Apostles' Creed is accepted by Catholics, Orthodox, and historically by the Anglicans, Lutherans, Reformed/ Presbyterians, Methodists, and Baptists. Most traditions require candidates for baptism to memorize it, believe it, and profess it aloud immediately before baptism.

Notably, heretical non-Trinitarian sects, such as the Mormons, Jehovah's Witnesses, and Oneness Pentecostals, reject the Apostles' Creed. While this book does not aim to settle doctrinal debates, it suggests that, historically speaking, and for the sake of the common good and cultural renewal, the Apostles' Creed can serve as a foundation for friendly cooperation.

The Apostles' Creed is the summary of the Good News (Gospel), and the bare minimum of Christian belief. It contains the doctrine of the Trinity, the essential biblical story of Christ's virgin birth, death, and resurrection, and the plan for forgiveness with life everlasting. However, salvation requires more than mere intellectual assent to the twelve doctrines of the Creed. Salvation and personal sanctification require an internal faith in the divine person and work of Christ. Satan knows every verse of the Bible and every line of the Apostles' Creed. He is not saved and never shall be saved.

PERSONAL FAITH AND DISCIPLESHIP

Memorizing the Gospel and Sacred Scripture does not necessarily yield personal salvation or sanctification. The Apostle James reminds us, "Thou believest that there is one God. Thou dost well. The devils also believe and tremble" (James 2:19). There must be a knowledge of faith and then a personal trust in our Lord Jesus Christ. One might know the definition of a chair, explain what a chair is, and even identify a chair. Sitting down in the chair with the belief that it will hold your weight is trust.

Trusting in Jesus Christ is moving beyond the doctrinal facts about Jesus Christ and placing the weight of our existence on His person and work of Jesus Christ. We place our sins upon Him by faith and confession. We place our hardships, trials, and worries upon Christ. This is living faith, and Saint Paul tells us that "faith working by love" is the only saving faith (Galatians 5:6). Faith must be coupled with hope and love: "And now there remain faith, hope, and love, these three: but the greatest of these is love" (1 Corinthians 13:13). Here Saint Paul uses the Greek word *agape* for love.

Agape is the Greek term used in the New Testament to describe a selfless, sacrificial, unconditional love. In Greek, it is the highest form of love, often associated with the love of God for His people and the love that Christians ought to have for one another. Saint John uses the word when he says, "God is love" (1 John 4:8). Unlike other Greek words for love, such as "eros" (love as desire) or "philia" (love as friendship), and "storge" (familial love), agape is not based on emotions but is an action of the will. Agape is love willing the betterment of the other. A faith in Christ that is not formed by agape for God and neighbor is not saving faith.

Our Lord Jesus Christ said, "If you love (*agapate*) me, keep my commandments. And I will ask the Father, and he shall give you another Paraclete, that he may abide with you forever" (John 14:15–16). If you have agape love for Christ, you must keep His commandments. Christianity is the grace of Christ, infusing faith that grows into action. So often we preach "faith in Christ" that we forget that "love for Christ" is higher. If we love Christ, He says we shall keep His commandments. I surveyed the teachings of Christ, and here are His commandments for us. As you read through them, inwardly reflect on how you can put Christ's teachings into practice:

1. Repent and believe the Good News (Matthew 4:17).
2. Hunger and thirst after righteousness (Matthew 5:6).
3. Show mercy (Matthew 5:7).
4. Make peace (Matthew 5:9).
5. Be glad and rejoice, for so they persecuted the prophets (Matthew 5:12).
6. Let your light shine before men (Matthew 5:16).
7. Make it right with an enemy. Then offer your gift to God (Matthew 5:24).
8. Try to reach a settlement (Matthew 5:25).
9. Turn the other cheek (Matthew 5:39).
10. Go the extra mile (Matthew 5:41).
11. Give to everyone who asks you for something (Matthew 5:42).
12. Love your enemies and treat well those who mistreat you, and bless those who curse you (Matthew 5:43).
13. Pray for those who abuse and persecute you (Matthew 5:44; Luke 6:27).
14. Be perfect (Matthew 5:48).
15. Give to the needy in secret (Matthew 6:2–4).
16. Pray to your Father in secret (Matthew 6:5–6).
17. Pray like this: "Our Father, who art in Heaven" (Matthew 6:9).
18. Forgive those who offend you (Matthew 6:14).
19. Fast in secret (Matthew 6:16–18).

20. Do no worry about your life, what you shall eat, nor for your body, what you shall put on (Matthew 6:25).
21. First seek the kingdom of God and his righteousness (Matthew 6:33; Luke 12:30).
22. Remove the plank from your own eye (Matthew 7:5).
23. Ask…seek…knock in prayer (Matthew 7:7).
24. Treat others in the way you yourself would like to be treated (Matthew 7:12).
25. Enter through the narrow gate (Matthew 7:13).
26. Beware of false prophets, who come to you in the clothing of sheep, but inwardly they are ravening wolves (Matthew 7:15).
27. Do what I say (Matthew 7:21).
28. Do what my heavenly Father desires (Matthew 7:21).
29. Hear and obey me (Matthew 7:24).
30. Go. Believe (Matthew 8:13).
31. Worship the Lord your God and serve Him only (Luke 4:8).
32. Make not my Fathers house into a market (John 2:16).
33. Worship God in spirit and in truth (John 4:24).
34. Do the will of him who sent me and accomplish his work (John 4:34).
35. See the fields. They are already ripe for harvest (John 4:36).
36. Come and follow me (Mark 1:17).
37. Be not afraid (Luke 5:10).

38. Take heart…your sins are forgiven (Mark 2:5; Matthew 9:2).
39. Learn what this means: "I desire mercy, not sacrifice" (Matthew 9:13).
40. Call sinners to repentance (Luke 5:32).
41. Do good on the Sabbath (Mark 3:5).
42. Exercise justice amongst the nations (Matthew 12:18).
43. Love much (Luke 7:47).
44. Go in peace (Luke 7:50).
45. First tie up the strong man (Matthew 12:29).
46. Gather with me (Matthew 12:30).
47. Hear the Word of God and do it (Luke 8:21).
48. Understand the parable(s) (Matthew 13:18).
49. Hear the Word, and understand it, and bear good fruit (Matthew 13:23).
50. Take heed therefore how you hear (Luke 8:18).
51. Go home to your relatives and tell them what great things the Lord God has done for you and how He had mercy on you (Mark 5:19).
52. Take heart (Matthew 9:22).
53. Go in peace, and be free from this affliction (Mark 5:34).
54. Stop weeping (Luke 8:52).
55. Get up. Pick up your mat and walk (John 5:8).
56. Come to me that you might have life (John 5:40).
57. Pray to the Lord of the harvest that He will send out workers into His harvest fields (Matthew 9:38).

58. Go to the lost sheep… (Matthew 10:6).
59. Say, "The kingdom of heaven has come" (Matthew 10:7).
60. Freely you have received, freely give (Matthew 10:8).
61. When you enter a city or village, find out who is worthy (Matthew 10:11).
62. When you enter the home, say a greeting (Matthew 10:12).
63. Shake off the dust from under your feet as a testimony (Matthew 10:14).
64. Be as wise as snakes and as gentle as doves (Matthew 10:16).
65. Do not fear them (Matthew 10:26).
66. Acknowledge me before others (Matthew 10:32).
67. Go and find out (Mark 6:38).
68. Bring the food here to me (Matthew 14:18).
69. Take courage. It is I (John 6:20).
70. Work…for the lasting food that gives eternal life (John 6:27).
71. Believe in the One whom He sent (John 6:29).
72. Come to me…believe in me…believe in the Son (John 6:35, 40, 47).
73. Eat my flesh…eat my body…drink my blood (John 6:5, 53–54, 58).
74. Come to me (John 6:37).
75. Eat the body of the Son of Man and drink His blood (John 6:53).

76. Watch out for the heresy of the Pharisees (Mark 8:15).
77. Judge not by the looks of things; judge rightly (John 7:24).
78. Come to me and drink (Isaiah 55:1; John 7:37).
79. Go your way and stop sinning (John 8:11).
80. Believe that I AM (John 8:24).
81. Continue in my word...be my disciples (John 8:31).
82. Take up your cross and follow me (Matthew 16:24).
83. Act on what I say (John 8:51).
84. Believe in the Son of God (John 9:35).
85. Believe the things I do (John 10:38).
86. Have faith the size of a mustard seed (Matthew 17:20).
87. Be last of all and servant of all (Mark 9:35).
88. Change your mind and become like little children (Matthew 18:2).
89. Humble yourselves (Matthew 18:4).
90. Listen carefully (Luke 9:44).
91. Be least amongst you (Luke 9:48).
92. Receive one such little child in my name (Mark 9:36).
93. Have salt amongst yourselves and live in peace with each other (Mark 9:50).
94. Go and tell him (offending brother) privately (Matthew 18:15).
95. Take one or two others with you (Matthew 18:16).
96. Tell it to the Church (Matthew 18:17).

97. Treat him as you would a pagan or a tax collector (Matthew 18:17).
98. Gather in my name (Matthew 18:20).
99. Forgive someone up to seventy times seven (Matthew 18:22).
100. Each of you, forgive your brother from your heart (Matthew 18:35).
101. Go out and announce the kingdom of God (Luke 9:60).
102. Earnestly ask the Lord of the harvest to send out workers into his harvest (Luke 10:2).
103. Rejoice that your names are recorded in heaven (Luke 10:20).
104. Standing to pray, having ought against another, forgive (Matthew 11:25).
105. Come to me, everyone who is weary and heavily laden (Matthew 11:28).
106. Put my yoke upon you and learn about me (Matthew 11:29).
107. Go and do the same (show mercy) (Luke 10:37).
108. Hear the Word of God and put it into practice (Luke 11:28).
109. Ensure that your body is full of light (Luke 11:36).
110. Give from the abundance of your heart (Luke 11:41).
111. Fear the One who can both kill you and throw you into hell. Yes, be afraid of Him (Luke 12:5).
112. Acknowledge me before men (Luke 12:8).

113. Watch out. Be on your guard against greed of all kinds (Luke 12:15).
114. Be rich toward God (Luke 12:21).
115. Sell your possessions and give to the poor. Provide money bags for yourselves that will not wear out (Luke 12:33).
116. Be dressed and ready, and keep your lamps burning. Be like those who are waiting for their master (Luke 12:35).
117. Be ready (Matthew 24:44).
118. Be a servant that watches...who is always ready (Luke 12:37–38).
119. Be a trustworthy and wise manager (Matthew 24:45).
120. Produce much...contribute much (Luke 12:48).
121. Try to enter through the narrow gate (Luke 13:24).
122. Say, "Blessed is the one who comes in the name of the Lord" (Luke 13:15).
123. Take the least important place (Luke 14:9).
124. Humble yourselves (Luke 14:11).
125. Invite the poor (Luke 14:12).
126. Compel the poor to come in (Luke 14:23).
127. "Hate" your family relative to Christ (Luke 14:26).
128. Sit down and count the cost (Luke 14:28).
129. Consider.... Ask for terms of peace (Luke 14:31–32).
130. Leave everything you have...be my disciple (Luke 14:33).
131. Search carefully until you find it (Luke 15:8).
132. Say "I have sinned against God and you; I am no longer worthy..." (Luke 15:18).

133. Use worldly wealth to make friends for yourselves (Luke 16:9).

134. Be faithful in the smallest things (Luke 16:10).

135. Listen to Moses and the prophets (Luke 16:31).

136. If your brother sins against you, rebuke him. If he repents, forgive him (Luke 17:4).

137. Say, "We are worthless servants who have only done our duty" (Luke 17:10).

138. Return and give glory to God (Luke 17:18).

139. Get up and go your way (Luke 17:19).

140. Cry out to God day and night (Luke 18:7).

141. Pray, "God, be merciful to me, for I am a sinner" (Luke 18:13).

142. Humble yourself (Luke 18:14).

143. What God has united, let no one pull apart (no divorce) (Mark 19:9).

144. Whoever can accept celibacy, let him accept it (Matthew 19:12).

145. Let the little children come to me and do not stop them (Mark 10:14).

146. Believe in me (John 11:25–26, 40).

147. Believe that the Father really sent me (John 11:42).

148. Obey the commandments (Matthew 19:17).

149. "Honor your father and mother" (Matthew 19:19; Luke 18:20).

150. "Love you neighbor as yourself" (Matthew 19:19).

151. Sell everything you have and give it to the poor (Matthew 19:21; Luke 18:22).

152. Take up the cross and follow me (Matthew 19:21).

153. Leave house or parents or...property (Matthew 19:29) .

154. Follow me (Matthew 19:28).

155. Drink the cup I drink (Matthew 20:23).

156. Be baptized with the baptism I undergo (Matthew 20:23).

157. Become a servant...the slave of all (Matthew 20:27–28; Mark 10:44).

158. Have faith in Jesus (Matthew 20:34; Luke 18:42).

159. Serve...give your life (Matthew 20:28; Mark 10:45).

160. Conduct business until I return (Luke 19:14).

161. Be a good servant...faithful in little things (Luke 19:17).

162. Leave her alone (Mark 14:6).

163. Recount what this woman has done (Matthew 26:23; Mark 14:9).

164. Call my house a house of prayer (Isaiah 56:7; Luke 19:46).

165. Praise from the mouths of babes and infants (Matthew 21:16).

166. Have faith.... Ask in prayer.... Truly believe (Matthew 21:21–22; Mark 11:24).

167. Listen to another parable (Matthew 21:33).

168. Respect the Son (Matthew 21:38).

169. Produce fruit for the kingdom (Matthew 21:43).

170. Read the Scriptures (Matthew 21:42).

171. Come to the wedding banquet (Matthew 22:4)

172. Invite anyone you find to the His feast (Matthew 22:9).

173. Give to Caesar what is Caesar's and to God what is God's (Mark 12:17; Luke 20:25).

174. Understand the Scriptures and the power of God (Matthew 22:29; Mark 12:24).

175. "Hear.... Love the Lord your God with all your heart, soul, mind and strength" (Deuteronomy 6:5; Matthew 22:37; Mark 12:29–30).

176. "Love your neighbor as yourself" (Matthew 22:39; Mark 12:30).

177. Do justice, mercy and faithfulness (Matthew 23:23).

178. First wash the inside of the cup and the disk (Matthew 23:26).

179. Say, "Blessed is the one who comes..." (Matthew 23:29).

180. Follow me.... Serve me (John 12:26).

181. Hate your life in this world (John 12:25).

182. Walk while you have the light.... Put your trust in the light while you have the light (John 12:25).

183. Turn around (John 12:40).

184. Believe in me and the one who sent me (John 12:44, 46).

185. Make sure you do not follow deceivers (Luke 21:8).

186. See to it that you are not disturbed (Matthew 24:6).

187. Testify before authorities and the nations (Matthew 10:18).

188. Settle it in your heart to ponder beforehand what to say (Luke 21:14).
189. Show a patient endurance (Matthew 10:22).
190. Flee to the mountains…run out of the city (Matthew 24:17).
191. Endure to the end (Matthew 24:13).
192. Preach this good news of the kingdom to all the world as a testimony to all peoples (Matthew 24:14).
193. Lift your heads and look up (Luke 21:28).
194. Learn…observe…know that the Kingdom is drawing nigh (Matthew 24:32–33).
195. Watch yourselves…. Make sure your hearts (Luke 21:34).
196. Watch and pray that you may have strength to escape (Luke 21:36).
197. Be careful. Keep watch…. (Luke 21:36, 25:13).
198. Come…inherit the Kingdom (Matthew 25:34).
199. Give food…give drink…welcome…clothe… visit…come to…the least esteemed of Jesus' brothers (Matthew 25:35–36, 40).
200. Call me Teacher and Lord (John 13:13).
201. Wash each other's feet (John 13:15).
202. Believe that I AM (John 13:19).
203. Welcome whomever I send…. Welcome me (John 13:20).
204. Believe that I am in the Father and the Father is in me (John 14:10).

205. Believe me that I am in the Father and that the Father is in me (John 14:11).

206. Ask anything using my name (John 14:13, 14).

207. Love me, keep my commandments (John 14:15).

208. Have my commandments and keep them (John 14:21).

209. Love me.... Keep my word (John 14:21, 23).

210. Abide in me (John 15:4).

211. Continue in my love (John 15:9).

212. Do everything I command you (John 15:14).

213. Love one another.(John 15:17).

214. Ask in my name (John 16:26).

215. Love me and believe that I came from God (John 16:27).

216. Take heart (John 16:33).

217. Do the will of God (John 17:17).

218. Put your faith in me (John 17:38).

219. Act on what I say (John 8:52).

220. Follow me and refuse to follow another (John 10:4–5).

221. Watch and pray that you may not be tempted (Mark 14:38).

222. Believe everything the prophets spoke (Luke 24:25).

223. Receive the Holy Spirit (John 20:22).

224. Go and make disciples of all peoples, baptizing them in the name of the Father, of the Son, and of the Holy Spirit, and teaching them to obey all that I commanded (Matthew 28:18–20).

We may debate constitutions, laws, and policies, but the commandments of our Lord Jesus Christ must be taught and received by His disciples. These are the recorded instructions of God for humanity. This is how a person is "transformed into the same image from glory to glory, as by the Spirit of the Lord" (2 Corinthians 3:18). We must obey these teachings before we seek to transform the rules and culture around us.

The temptation of the Christian Patriot is to perceive cultural transformation as a legal imposition. Christ our Lord provided the precise way in which the kingdom of heaven transforms humanity: "The kingdom of heaven is like to leaven, which a woman took and hid in three measures of meal, until the whole was leavened" (Matthew 13:33).

EVANGELIZE YOUR FAMILY

From the overflow of the heart, the mouth speaks. The family is the basic unit of society, and it is normally the basic unit of God's blessing. God changed the name of Abram to Abraham, meaning "exalted father," and promised: "In thee shall all the families of the earth be blessed" (Genesis 12:3). The family is the natural and normative way that faith is passed from one generation to the next. Not everyone is blessed with good Christian parents, and people come to faith in a variety of ways, but the story of the Old Testament and Christian history reveal that faith is typically planted in the family. When the Apostle Peter preached his first sermon on Pentecost, he concluded by saying, "This promise [salvation] is to you and your children" (Acts 2:39). The parental task to catechize and evangelize our children is rooted in Deuteronomy 6:6–7: "These words that I command you today shall be on your heart. You shall teach them diligently to your children." Later in Proverbs 22:6, we read: "Train up a child in the way he should go; even when he is old he will not depart from it."

The Bible places significant responsibility on fathers to instill faith. Ephesians 6:4 instructs, "Fathers, do not provoke your children to anger, but bring them up in the discipline and instruction of the Lord." Joshua exemplifies this, declaring, "As for me and my house, we will serve the Lord" (Joshua 24:15), binding his family to faith through his leadership. Fathers often shirk their spiritual power and authority and offload it onto their wives. This is a dreadful mistake on the part of husbands. Original sin occurred when Adam took a passive role and allowed his wife Eve to dialogue with the serpent. Men must not abandon their ministerial role in the home.

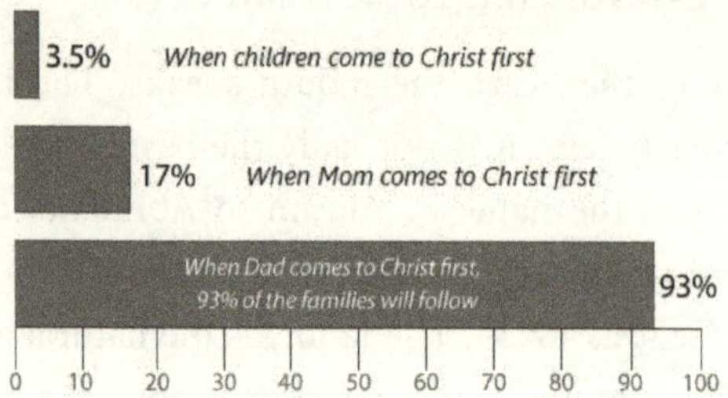

Haggerty, Justin. "Catholic Fatherhood: Fathers Lead Families to Christ." *Knights Republic.* April 17, 2021. https://www.knightsrepublic.com/single-post/catholic-fatherhood-fathers-lead-families-to-christ.

A 2021 Barna Group study found that 68 percent of children raised by actively religious fathers (determined as attending church weekly) grew up to identify as Christian adults. Compare 68 percent with 42 percent of children who grew up with fathers who did not attend church weekly. Another study revealed similar data. When the father and mother attended church, 72 percent of children remained faithful into adulthood. When the father alone attended church, 55 percent of children remained faithful. When the mother alone attended church without the father, only 15 percent remained faithful! When neither attended church, only 6 percent of the children remained faithful. A similar study revealed that when a father comes to Christ, 93 percent of families follow his lead. When a mother converts, only 17 percent of families follow.

INFLUENCE OF PARENTS ATTENDING CHURCH ON FAITH OF CHILDREN

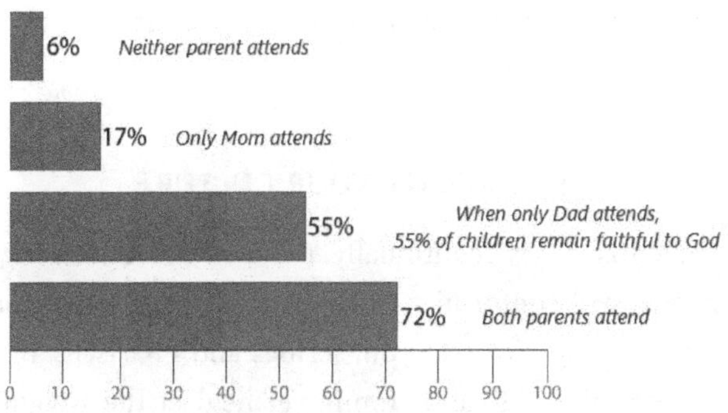

Bruce, Robert G., and Debra Fulghum Bruce. *Becoming Spiritual Soulmates with Your Child.* Nashville, TN: Broadman & Holman Publishers, 1996.

There are social reasons for these outcomes, but rooted deeply in the phenomenon is that God is our "Father," and the father provides the clearest expression of God's love, justice, and mercy for the family.

The outcomes are not assured. Children can reject faith, as seen with Eli's sons (1 Samuel 2:12). Still, a Christian father's consistent witness, rooted in love (1 Corinthians 13:7), maximizes the likelihood of children remaining faithful. Men, in particular, are tasked with evangelizing their families for multiple generations. Thus, if a father is a Christian, his children are often Christian too—not infallibly, but through biblical duty, covenantal grace, and lived example.

The family should be catechized by daily prayer (morning and evening) and prayers before meals. Catechism classes, Sunday school, and religious schools are necessary but should never relieve the parents of their task in ensuring the proper Christian education of their children. The Catholic, Orthodox, and many Protestant religions have an annual liturgical calendar that carries us through the life of Christ (Christmas through Easter), and they provide a yearly course in Christian education. The home should be a "domestic church" and the cathedral of Christian love. Saint John Chrysostom urges, "Let us make our homes churches" (Homily on Ephesians 20).

EVANGELIZE YOUR CULTURE

Our Lord Jesus Christ continually rebuked the Pharisees for prioritizing outward conformity to the law over the inner conversion of the heart, saying: "Woe to you, scribes and Pharisees, hypocrites! For you tithe mint, dill, and cumin, yet neglect the weightier matters of the law: justice, mercy, and faith. These things you ought to have done, without neglecting the others" (Matthew 23:23). The evangelization of culture does not focus on enforcing outward conformity. Instead, it aims to transform people into Christian saints, enabling society to rise with the faith and love of its people.

There are estimated to be 2.6 billion Christians in this world of 8 billion people. If each of the 2.6 billion deeply converted to Christ and His Church *and subsequently led three people to Christ*, they entire world would be Christian. How then do we lead people to Christ? When Andrew met Jesus, "he found first his brother Simon, and said to him: We have found the Messiah, which is, being interpreted, the Christ" (John 1:41). That's the basis for evangelizing culture.

culture. Go and tell other people: "I have found Jesus Christ. He has changed my life. I want you to meet Him too."

Some people worry that they are not educated enough or holy enough to share their faith in Christ with others. Be not afraid. You will not have all the answers, and the best course is to say, "I don't know the answer to that, but I will try to find it for you." Initially, however, the best witness is to explain how Christ has transformed your personally. The Ivy League atheist cannot punch holes in your experience. Your life in Christ stands on its own. Regarding being holy enough, be not afraid. Confess that you are a sinner and unworthy. Often, nonbelievers are put off by those wearing a mask of false piety. Be vulnerable and be honest. You are not trying to win them to yourself, but to Christ.

Encourage friendly conversations. Offer them books. Share videos. Invite them to prayer groups or Bible studies. Ask them to attend church. Introduce them to your pastor. Stay engaged. Saying, "I will be praying for you," or "Would you like to come to church with me this Sunday?" is often all it takes. The transformation of culture begins with the inward transformation of millions of people. Christ commanded us for this task:

> And Jesus coming, spoke to them, saying: All power is given to me in heaven and in earth. Going therefore, teach ye all nations; baptizing them in the name of the Father, and of the Son, and of the Holy Ghost. Teaching them to observe all things whatsoever I have commanded you: and behold I am with you all days, even to the consummation of the world (Matthew 28:18–20).

STRATEGY 2

TAKE UP PUBLIC SPACE FOR CHRIST

Just as we seek to fill the ranks of Christ's one Church with fervent believers eager to transform the world for Christ as our King, the New Secular Religion aims for the same objective. The New Secular Religion seeks to dominate our minds by controlling public and civil spaces. Pride parades on Main Street, drag queens in public libraries, a Black Lives Matter Plaza in front of the White House, and statues of the demon Baphomet in courthouses act as incursions into civic spaces to establish their ideology as standard and acceptable.

Their strategy is an inverted perversion of what God intended from the beginning. Since the days of Adam, humans have honored God through physical monuments, altars, arks, pillars, and temples. These public structures established the civic foundation for Christian civilization. Christian emperors, kings, guilds, and paupers erected raised crosses, statues, tombs, and breath-taking basilicas to glorify their triune God.

THE PROBLEM OF SECULAR MONUMENTS

I recall visiting the Lincoln Memorial as a young man and being perplexed by its inscription: "In this temple, as in the hearts of the people for whom he saved the union, the memory of Abraham

Lincoln is enshrined forever." There sat Abraham Lincoln, silently enthroned like Jupiter, chiseled in white marble quarried from Georgia. "This," I thought to myself, "should not be a *temple*."

A similar political deification can be seen in the impressive fresco of *The Apotheosis of George Washington*, located inside the United States Capitol. Painted by Italian artist Constantino Brumidi in 1865, the fresco embellishes the interior of the Capitol dome's canopy and is 180 feet above the rotunda floor. The Greek term "apotheosis" comes from "apo-" (which means "away from" or "to make separate") and "theos" (which means "god"). Literally, apotheosis translates to "making into a god" or "deification."

The ancient Greeks applied apotheosis to mortals like Hercules and Asclepius, who became gods. Alexander the Great co-opted the idea and applied it to himself, insinuating that he had been deified. The ancient Romans applied it to their founder, Romulus. After the assassination of Julius Caesar in 44 BC, a comet appeared during his funeral games. His adopted son, Augustus Caesar, interpreted the omen as his apotheosis and declared him "Divine Julius," building a temple in the Forum. This set a precedent for all future Roman Emperors until Constantine.

The Temple of Lincoln and *The Apotheosis of Washington* illustrate a tendency in American culture to deify the Founding Fathers, while we do not publicly honor the God who truly endowed us with the rights to life, liberty, and the pursuit of happiness. There is no theological justification for a civil monument to George Washington's apotheosis in our Capitol building; it highlights the lack of genuine piety in the United States. What we truly need are public monuments honoring God.

BIBLICAL MONUMENTS BUILT TO HONOR GOD

The Bible recounts numerous instances where God's people built physical markers to recognize His presence, power, or promises. These objects were not just utilitarian but served as sacred symbols of covenant and praise. Here are some of the most significant examples:

1. **Noah's Altar after the Flood**

   After surviving the deluge, Noah's first act on dry land was to build an altar. Genesis 8:20 states, "And Noah built an altar unto the Lord: and taking of all cattle and fowls that were clean, offered holocausts upon the altar."

2. **Abraham's Altars of Covenant**

   Abraham, called by God to a land of promise, repeatedly built altars to commemorate divine encounters. In Genesis 12:7, after God pledged Canaan to his descendants, "And the Lord appeared to Abram, and said to him: To thy seed will I give this land. And he built there an altar to the Lord, who had appeared to him." Later, in Genesis 13:18, "Abram removed his tent, and came, and dwelt by the vale of Mambre...and he built there an altar to the Lord." These altars, likely unadorned heaps of stone, stood as testaments to God's faithfulness and Abraham's trust, sanctifying the land with worship.

3. **Jacob's Stone at Bethel**

   Jacob's dream of a ladder to heaven prompted a monument of remembrance. Genesis 28:18–19 records, "And Jacob, rising up in the morning, took the stone, which he had laid under his head, and set it up for a title, pouring oil upon the top of it. And he called the name of that place Bethel, that is, the house of God." This anointed pillar honored God's revelation and promise, transforming a humble stone into a sacred marker. Later, in Genesis 35:14, "He set up also a monument of stone, in the place where God had spoken to him: pouring drink offerings upon it, and pouring oil thereon," reinforcing Bethel's sanctity.

4. **The Ark of the Covenant**

   Under Moses' leadership, the Israelites crafted the Ark as a portable throne for God's presence. Exodus 25:10–11 commands, "Frame an ark of setim wood...and thou shalt overlay it with the purest gold within and without." Adorned with cherubim and housing the tablets of the Law, it symbolized God's covenant and holiness. Carried through the wilderness, the Ark was a dynamic monument, honoring God as their guide and protector.

5. **The Twelve Stones at Gilgal**

   After crossing the Jordan River into the Promised Land, Joshua erected a monument of twelve stones, one for each tribe. Joshua 4:20–21 recounts, "And the twelve stones, which they had taken out of the channel of the Jordan, Joshua pitched in Gilgal, and said to the children of Israel: When your children shall ask their fathers tomorrow, saying: 'What mean these stones?'" This circle of stones honored God's miraculous provision, a teaching tool for future generations about His power.

6. **The Temple of Solomon**

   The pinnacle of biblical architecture, Solomon's Temple was a grand edifice built to house God's glory. 1 Kings

6:1–2 describes its inception: "And it came to pass in the four hundred and eightieth year after the children of Israel came out of Egypt...that Solomon began to build a house to the Lord." Adorned with gold, cedar, and stone, it replaced the portable Tabernacle, fulfilling David's vision. 1 Kings 8:10–11 notes, "The cloud filled the house of the Lord. And the priests could not stand to minister...for the glory of the Lord had filled the house." This temple stood as the ultimate monument to God's presence among His people.

These biblical structures—altars, stones, arks, and temples—served as intergenerational signposts pointing to the providential greatness of Almighty God. They bridged the divine and human, a tradition that Christianity would build upon in the centuries to come.

CHRISTIAN MONUMENTS TO CHRIST

After Christ's resurrection, the focus of worship shifted from a single temple to a universal Church. Over the past 2,000 years, Christians have built awe-inspiring monuments—crosses, tombs, and cathedrals—to glorify God and proclaim His Son's redemptive work. Below are several standout examples across time and geography.

Beginning in the catacombs, Christians covertly marked their places and residences with crosses, fishes, and the name of Jesus Christ. After the conversion of Constantine, the cross and the name of Jesus Christ were emblazoned on their military standards, courthouses, plazas, and public buildings. Bible verses were also inscribed publicly, and this tradition lived on into the modern era where the Ten Commandments were engraved as the code of justice in our courthouses and schools.

Constantine transformed the tradition of Roman emperors claiming divinity for themselves. Previously, emperors commissioned public monuments to preserve and "deify" their personas and accomplishments. Instead, Constantine allocated public funds to build monuments in honor of Christ and His Apostles. His reign marked the beginning of grand Christian construction projects that not only symbolized a shift away from paganism but also laid the physical foundations for Christianity's dominance in Western civilization. Constantine's architectural efforts—churches, basilicas, and memorials—reflected his personal conversion, political strategy, and vision for a unified empire under a single God.

Constantine's conversion to Christianity famously began with his victory at the Battle of Milvian Bridge in AD 312. According to Eusebius of Caesarea, Constantine saw a vision of a cross in the sky with the words, "In this sign, you will conquer." After triumphing under the Christian symbol of the Chi-Rho (the first two letters of CHRist in Greek), he issued the Edict of Milan in AD 313 with Licinius, granting religious tolerance to Christians. This newfound freedom spurred Constantine to sponsor building projects that would glorify Christ and legitimize his rule as divinely ordained.

His earliest and most significant project was the Church of the Holy Resurrection in Jerusalem, known today as the Holy Sepulcher. Built over the presumed sites of Jesus' crucifixion and empty tomb as identified by Constantine's mother, Helena, during her 326–328 pilgrimage, the complex was a bold architectural statement of Christian triumph in the Holy Land. Dedicated around 335, it featured a rotunda over the empty tomb, a basilica (civic hall for gatherings), and a courtyard enclosing Golgotha for Christians to gather. Constantine lavishly funded the project, using imperial resources to excavate and construct the church with imported marble and gold mosaics.

In Rome, Constantine repurposed imperial architecture for Christian worship with the Basilica of St. Peter. Begun around 324 on Vatican Hill, Constantine replaced a modest brick shrine built over the burial site of the Apostle Peter. The new church built over the tomb of Peter included a five-aisled basilica, 350 feet long, adorned with marble columns and a wooden roof. Constantine's project signaled that Rome no longer honored the Caesars who killed Christians but honored the fisherman who once walked on water with Christ. Peter had been killed outside the Roman walls at the bottom of the Vatican Hill, and this location, now called the Vatican, became the spiritual heart of the city.

Under Constantine, the Basilica of Saint John Lateran became Rome's first official cathedral after Constantine donated the Lateran Palace to Bishop Miltiades around AD 313. Prior to this, Christians worshipped secretly in the catacombs and covertly in homes that had been converted into churches. Constantine desired to provide Rome with its first cathedral dedicated to public worship. He gifted one of the most desirable pieces of real estate in Rome for this purpose, the Lateran Basilica, which provided an enormous rectangular hall and apse for congregations to gather. The original wooden table that had been used by Saint Peter was encased in marble and set up as the altar of the basilica.

Nearby, Constantine commissioned the Church of the Holy Cross in Rome. His mother, Saint Helena, credited with finding the True Cross at Golgotha, returned not only with relics but also with soil from the site of the crucifixion. Tradition holds that Constantine brought back a ship's worth of dirt from Jerusalem for the church's foundation, allowing those who walk there to be "walking in the Holy Land" of Christ.

Beyond Rome and Jerusalem, Constantine founded Constantinople (modern Istanbul) in AD 330 as a "New Rome," embedding

Christianity at its core. The Church of the Holy Apostles, initiated during his reign and completed by his (wayward) son Constantius II, housed his tomb amid apostolic relics, blending imperial and sacred authority. The cruciform shape of the church influenced Byzantine architecture, while the Hagia Irene (Holy Peace), an early cathedral, demonstrated his commitment to a Christian capital. In this first "Christian planned" city, the cathedral—rather than the courthouse or emperor's residence—served as the central focus of Christian society. Christian cities from this period would position the cathedral, church, or chapel at the heart of the city, expanding outward from there. The church, not the king, became the symbolic heart of the city.

PUBLIC CROSSES AND STATUES OF CHRIST

Visitors to Europe have observed crosses and monuments to Christ, the Virgin Mary, and local saints that are visible on nearly every street corner and plaza. Churches and chapels are open throughout the day, beckoning Christians to stop and pray. Having grown up in Texas, I have observed similar sights in my home state. The largest cross in America is the Corpus Christi Cross in Corpus Christi, Texas, standing at 230 feet. There is also a 190-foot-tall cross standing in Groom, Texas, surrounded by bronze versions of the Stations of the Cross. It creates a significant visual and spiritual landmark, drawing visitors from around the world. Ballinger, Texas, has a hundred-foot cross with a seventy-foot wingspan. There is also the seventy-seven-foot Kerrville Cross in the Texas Hill Country, featuring seventy-seven Bible verses engraved in stone.

These local monuments publicly speak to the faith of the local people: "From the overflow of the heart, the mouth speaks" (Matthew 12:34). While some cities promote or tolerate pride flags and parades, other cities promote Christ as King and Christ first. A new emphasis is growing across the world to reclaim our public space for Christ. In the last several decades, new monuments have been erected to publicly acknowledge Christ as King.

High above Rio de Janeiro, atop Mount Corcovado in Tijuca National Park, stands *Christ the Redeemer,* a monumental statue of Jesus Christ that has watched over the city since its unveiling on October 12, 1931. Rising 38 meters (125 feet) from its base, this Art Deco icon stretches its arms 28 meters wide, embracing the sprawling beaches and mountains below. Completed after nearly a decade of work that began in 1922, it remains one of the world's most celebrated landmarks with the message that Christ is the Redeemer of mankind.

The statue's creation stemmed from a post-World War I vision of peace. Designed by Heitor da Silva Costa and Carlos Oswald, with Paul Landowski sculpting its serene face and hands, it was built using reinforced concrete and clad in durable soapstone. Funded by donations through Semana do Monumento, construction cost $250,000, a testament to collective faith in Jesus Christ. Dedicated in 1931 by President Getúlio Vargas, its electric lights were famously switched on from Rome. It's about time that a site of Christian heritage was named one of the New Seven Wonders of the World in 2007.

Likewise, Samosir Island in Indonesia just recently built the tallest monument to Jesus Christ known to man, reaching 200 feet (61 meters). Unveiled on September 19, 2024, the world's tallest statue of Jesus Christ overlooks Lake Toba in North Sumatra, a region with a significant Christian minority. Crafted by artists Himawan and Eko, it was commissioned by the local Catholic community, funded through donations totaling roughly $330,000. Its recent completion marks it as a symbol of contemporary Christian outreach in a predominantly Muslim nation.

Similarly (but not as tall), is *Christ the King* in Świebodzin, Poland, at 170 feet (52.5 meters), completed on November 6, 2010. Conceived by retired priest Sylwester Zawadzki, this statue was a grassroots effort, funded by $1.5 million in donations from the town's 21,000 residents. Zawadzki envisioned it as a declaration of faith, with its 33-meter figure symbolizing Jesus' earthly lifespan. The statue's construction reflects Poland's deep Christian roots, aiming to assert spiritual identity in a post-communist era and draw pilgrims to an otherwise unremarkable town.

Another example of taking up Christian space in a Muslim nation is *Christ Blessing the World* in Manado, Indonesia, completed in 2007 and standing 160 feet (50 meters) tall. Local Christian real estate mogul Ir. Ciputra, inspired while standing on the hill with his wife in the early 2000s, funded its $540,000 cost. The monument—tilted 20 degrees forward—embodies a blessing over the Christian community below, who live as minorities in a Muslim nation. These monuments are outward signs of an inward reality: this is a Christian place. The people here honor Christ as their king.

NATIONAL RECOGNITION OF CHRIST AS KING

Taking up space for Christ is not just about building crosses, churches, and monuments. It can also take the form of political actions. We often think of European nations as having been ruled by kings. Poland took it to the next level and legally declared Jesus Christ as its king in a symbolic and religious ceremony on November 19, 2016. This event, known as the "Jubilee Act of Acceptance of Jesus Christ as King and Lord," took place at the Church of Divine Mercy in Kraków, a city deeply tied to Poland's Christian history. The nation made a spiritual declaration that it belonged to Jesus Christ and that He is their true king. The event was attended by thousands, including Polish President Andrzej Duda, Catholic bishops and clergy, and the laity, marking a significant moment of national religious expression.

The declaration commemorated the 1,050th anniversary of Poland's first baptisms in AD 966 under Mieszko I, which traditionally marks the country's Christianization. During the ceremony, Cardinal Stanisław Dziwisz recited a prayer that acknowledged Christ's reign: "Immortal King of Ages Lord Jesus Christ, our God and Savior...we Poles stand in front of you...to acknowledge your reign, surrender to Thy law, entrust and take you to our homeland and the whole nation." This act was framed as a collective submission to Christ's spiritual authority, not a political enthronement, as Bishop Andrzej Czaja later clarified that the event was not to limit Christ as merely the King of Poland: "It is not a declaration of Christ the King of Poland. His kingdom is not of this earth." The prayer also invoked Christ's rule over families, schools, and the nation, echoing Pope Pius XI's 1925 encyclical *Quas Primas,* which established the Feast of Christ the King to assert Christ's universal sovereignty. Thus, Poland's declaration of Christ as king on November 19, 2016, was a ceremonial reaffirmation of faith, driven by historical devotion, national pride, and a desire to spiritually renew the country rather than a shift to theocracy. Its timing and scale made it a striking public testament to Poland's enduring religious character. Christian Patriots should seek to reach levels of influence and majority to make public actions like this common throughout Christian nations of the world.

CONFESSIONAL STATES

Confessional Christian nations currently exist throughout the world. A confessional nation is one that officially confesses Jesus Christ. Several nations publicly recognize Jesus Christ as their sovereign in their constitutions and governmental documents, such as:

- Armenia
- Greece
- Denmark
- United Kingdom
- Norway
- Iceland
- Malta
- Monaco
- Liechtenstein
- Costa Rica
- Argentina
- Zambia
- Tuvalu
- Samoa

If there are Muslim and Jewish states, there can be Christian nations. If a nation is truly the collection of family units and those family units are Christian, then naming Jesus Christ as Lord, Savior, Redeemer, and King in government documents is perfectly justified and brings honor and glory to God.

From the stone pillars of the patriarchs to the two-hundred-foot crosses across Texas, monuments to God span the sacred and the tangible. In the Bible, they serve as memorials for the people of God to remember His mercies. In the Christian era, they proclaim Christ's victory—crosses piercing the sky, statues embracing the world, cathedrals echoing with prayer. Each structure, whether ancient or modern, fulfills Psalm 28:2: "Bring to the Lord glory and honor: bring to the Lord glory to His name."

ACTION ITEMS FOR CHRISTIAN NATIONHOOD

1. Christians should "take up space" by displaying signs of Christian patrimony. Crosses, the Ten Commandments, churches, chapels, Bible verses, statues, and public monuments can and should be set up in private and public spaces.
2. Christians should lead public acts of consecration or dedication of their families, town, states, and nations to Jesus Christ as King.
3. Christians should endeavor to establish confessional Christian nations and defend the status of those that already are.

STRATEGY 3

DEFINE MATRIMONY

"The family is the cell of resistance to the state."

—G.K. Chesterton, *The Man Who Was Thursday*

The Book of Genesis begins with the creation and institution of holy matrimony—a sacred covenantal bond between husband and wife. Marriage is a creation ordinance of God that binds man and woman together for mutual benefit and the procreation and education of children. Marriage is the building block of society and the political nation.

In his "Letter to the People of the United States," George Washington stated, "The well-being of society is based on the family, and the welfare of the family is essential to the well-being of the nation." The second president of the United States, John Adams, stated, "The foundation of society is laid in the marriage bond."[1] Our first two presidents established this conviction directly from Genesis. However, it does not take the Holy Bible to come to this conclusion. Several centuries before Christ, the Greek philosopher Aristotle affirmed the same truth from the Natural Law written in his heart: "The family is the association established by nature for the supply of man's everyday wants."[2]

Any law, policy, or agency that does not recognize John Adams's teaching that "the foundation of society is laid in the marriage bond" should be vigorously resisted and attacked by Christians. And the "marriage bond" is not a man-made concept that can be arbitrarily redefined by Congress, the Supreme Court, or an executive order. The marriage bond was instituted by God the Creator in Genesis and later defined by our Lord Jesus Christ: "From the beginning of the creation, God made them male and female" (Mark 10:6).

THE LEGAL DEFINITION OF MATRIMONY

Christians should insist that matrimony be legally defined in the United States and in every nation of the world. The proper language should be something similar to this:

> MATRIMONY or MARRIAGE is the monogamous union of a biological man and biological woman having reached the age of majority. Marriage is rendered valid and binding when the man and woman make vows of their own free volition, without compulsion, to form a legal and spiritual bond "until death do us part."

Marriage must be defined accurately because God is the only one who defines it. If atheists or secularists deny God, then they also deny marriage as defined by God. We should not allow them to define the institution of marriage, which has been created by God and affirmed by Jesus Christ. We have the unbroken legal precedent of every Western nation for the last thousand years on our side, along with the Founding Fathers of the United States, our Founding Documents, "nature's laws," and the teachings of the Old and New Testaments. Here are some historical examples:

The Theodosian Code is the first historical example of Christians introducing Christian matrimony into Roman Law as a legally *and morally*-binding union.[3] Ratified by the Christian emperor Theodosian II around AD 483, it introduces the legal requirement for a heterosexual union and insists on mutual consent by the man and woman in the vows. Whereas previous Roman law did not require mutual consent (female consent was undervalued), the Theodosian Code required mutual consent by *both* the groom and the bride. Parental approval was required if the parties were under legal age. This Christian definition also prohibited marriage between close relatives, contrary to previous Roman custom, which allowed cousins to marry. This was the first introduction of laws against incest. Certain marriages were forbidden between Roman citizens of vastly different social statuses. For example, Roman senators were prohibited from marrying prostitutes or theater actresses.

Adultery was criminalized by law and heavily punished in order to protect the ideal of marital fidelity between husband and wife.[4] Before the Theodosian Code, divorce was easily obtained within Roman, pagan, and Jewish jurisprudence. Our Lord Jesus Christ prohibited divorce strictly—so strictly that his apostles were stunned:

> "And there came to him the Pharisees tempting him, saying: 'Is it lawful for a man to put away his wife for every cause?'
>
> He answering, said to them: 'Have ye not read, that he who made man from the beginning, made them male and female?' And he said: For this cause shall a man leave father and mother, and shall cleave to his wife, and they two shall be in one flesh. Therefore now they are not two, but one flesh. What therefore God hath joined together, let no man put asunder'" (Matthew 19:3–6).

> When asked why Moses permitted divorce, Jesus responded: "Moses, because of the hardness of your hearts, permitted you to put away your wives: but from the beginning it was not so. And I say to you, that whosoever shall put away his wife, except it be for fornication, and shall marry another, committeth adultery" (Matthew 19:8–9).

Elsewhere, Christ taught:

> "Whosoever shall put away his wife and marry another, committeth adultery against her. And if the wife shall put away her husband, and be married to another, she committeth adultery" (Mark 10:11–12).

Christ's strong position on divorce and adultery reflects the divine prohibition found in the Ten Commandments: "Thou shalt not commit adultery" (Exodus 20:14). Since Jews did not accept the teaching of Jesus Christ on divorce and adultery, the Theodosian Code prohibited marriage between Christians and Jews.[5] Furthermore, if a divorce was deemed unjust, the guilty party could lose their property or be penalized. If the husband committed adultery or abandoned his wife, he was required to provide financial support if the marriage ended through no fault of the wife.[6] Laws were also introduced to protect the chastity of young women, reflecting Christian values about purity. Severe penalties were imposed on anyone who seduced or abducted a virgin.[7]

THE DANGER OF NO-FAULT DIVORCE

The history of no-fault divorce represents a significant cultural and legal shift against the Christian tradition of marriage and family. From a Christian perspective, marriage is not merely a social contract but a sacred covenant established by God. Civil divorce was traditionally viewed as a last resort based on a severe and dangerous fault that endangered one spouse or the children. The introduction of no-fault divorce in 1969 in the United Sates not only changed civil law but also challenged long-standing Christian principles about the permanence of marriage, leading to widespread debate within Christian communities.

For centuries, Christianity has upheld marriage as a divine institution rooted in Scripture. Jesus' teachings on marriage are clear and uncompromising. In the Gospel of Matthew, Jesus states: "What therefore God hath joined together, let not man put asunder" (Matthew 19:6). Furthermore, Jesus allowed divorce only in cases of adultery (Matthew 19:9) and emphasized that remarriage after divorce constituted adultery. The Apostle Paul echoed these teachings, affirming the sacredness of marriage and urging Christians to remain faithful to their spouses (1 Corinthians 7:10–11).

For most of Western history, these biblical principles shaped the legal and cultural understanding of marriage. Divorce was seen as a grave failure, permitted only in extreme cases such as adultery, abandonment, or abuse. Even when civil law allowed for divorce, it was often accompanied by social stigma, especially within Christian communities. Marriage was not simply a contract between two individuals but a covenant before God with moral and spiritual implications.

The cultural and legal shift toward no-fault divorce began in the mid-20th century. Prior to this, divorce in America was largely fault-based, meaning one spouse had to prove that the other had committed a serious offense such as adultery, physical violence, or desertion. The legal system often encouraged false accusations and staged evidence to meet the legal criteria for divorce. This situation created a significant burden for couples seeking to end irreparably broken marriages.

The Family Law Act of 1969 in California, regrettably signed by then-Governor Ronald Reagan (who had married a divorced woman), introduced the concept of no-fault divorce. The Family Law Act allowed couples to divorce based on "irreconcilable differences" without the need to prove fault or wrongdoing by either party. This new law marked a dramatic departure from centuries of the Christian legal tradition that saw no-fault divorce as an erosion of the biblical teaching of the Holy Bible and the direct words of our Lord Jesus Christ. Ronald Reagan later expressed regret for signing the law, acknowledging that it inadvertently contributed to the rise in divorce rates and the weakening of the family unit. From a Christian perspective, this moment in history is seen as the beginning of a broader cultural movement that prioritized individual autonomy over covenantal commitments.

THE SPREAD OF NO-FAULT DIVORCE

Following California's lead, other states quickly adopted no-fault divorce laws. By the mid-1970s, no-fault divorce was the norm across much of the country. By 1985, every state except South Dakota had some form of no-fault divorce. New York was the last state to adopt it in 2010.

No-fault divorce was initially seen as a progressive and liberal reform that would reduce conflict, streamline the legal process, and protect the dignity of both spouses. However, from a Christian perspective, this legal change brought unintended consequences. Many Christian leaders and theologians argued that no-fault divorce undermined the seriousness of marital vows and made divorce too accessible, contributing to the breakdown of the family.

While states and nations began to legalize no-fault divorce, Pope John Paul II set pen to paper to condemn it. In his 1984 *Letter to Families,* he emphasized the indissolubility of marriage and expressed concern about new no-fault laws that made it easier for married couples to pursue divorce. He prophetically concluded that the legal changes for no-fault divorce would erode the West's definition of the family: "A broken family can, for its part, consolidate a specific form of 'anti-civilization,' destroying love in its various expressions, with inevitable consequences for the whole of life in society."[8]

As more no-fault divorce laws were passed, divorce rates soared in the 1970s and 1980s, reaching historically high levels. While some scholars debate whether no-fault divorce directly caused this increase, it undoubtedly played a role in reshaping societal attitudes toward marriage and divorce. From a Christian perspective, the consequences of this shift were deeply troubling. Marriage, once viewed as a lifelong covenant "till death do us part," became increasingly seen as a temporary financial arrangement subject to personal preferences and circumstances. The following effects are particularly significant:

1. **Single Parent Homes**

   Christian civilizations believe the family is the cornerstone of society. The rise in divorce rates following the no-fault revolution contributed to an increase in single-parent households, which many argue weakened the stability of family life. Scripture emphasizes the importance of family unity and the role of parents in raising children in the faith (Deuteronomy 6:6–7; Ephesians 6:4). Broken marriages often disrupt this biblical model.

2. **Wounds for Children**

   One of the most significant concerns among Christians has been the impact of no-fault divorce on children. Research shows that children from divorced families are more likely to experience emotional and psychological difficulties, lower academic performance, and struggles with relationships in adulthood. Christians emphasize the importance of protecting and nurturing children, viewing the family as a God-ordained environment for their growth and development.

3. **Marriage as Contract, not Covenant**

   Theologically, no-fault divorce represents a shift from a covenantal view of marriage to a contractual one. In a covenantal marriage, the relationship is grounded in mutual sacrifice, faithfulness, and God's design. The bride and groom are united spiritually and physically for life by God—not by the State. No-fault divorce, by contrast, treats marriage as a private contract that can be dissolved at will—like a business contract. This change is seen as a direct challenge to biblical teachings on the sanctity and permanence of marriage.

Christian leaders and denominations have responded to the rise of no-fault divorce in various ways. Some have called for a return to biblical principles, urging couples to prioritize reconciliation and counseling over divorce. Others have focused on strengthening marriage preparation and providing pastoral care for struggling couples. Several Christian organizations have also engaged in political advocacy, promoting policies that support marriage and family stability. These efforts have included campaigns to promote covenant marriage laws, which require couples to undergo counseling and agree to stricter divorce conditions. Nearly all Christian communities have also recognized the need for grace and compassion in dealing with the realities of divorce. As far back as the Theodosian Code, the legal separation of spouses is permitted when one spouse makes the living arrangement impossible due to violence or abandonment. While upholding the sanctity of marriage, Christians have sought to support divorced individuals and families, acknowledging that God's grace is sufficient for all situations.

The "free pass" to walk away from marriage for "irreconcilable differences" is entirely contrary to Genesis, the teaching of Christ, and the consensus of the New Testament. While no-fault divorce addressed some legitimate concerns about the limitations of fault-based divorce, it also opened the door to a more casual approach to ending marriages, which many Christians see as inconsistent with biblical teaching.

From a Christian perspective, the response to no-fault divorce should not be one of condemnation, but rather a renewed commitment to God's design for marriage. This means supporting couples in their commitment, offering grace and healing to those who have experienced divorce, and calling society back to a higher vision of marriage—one rooted in love, sacrifice, and covenantal faithfulness. It may seem impossible to restore the previous laws regulating marriage, but we can no longer treat marriage as an "at-will" business contract.

HOMOSEXUAL UNIONS CAN NEVER BE "MARRIAGE"

If holy matrimony as defined by God is a lifelong, exclusive covenant between one man and one woman, ordered toward the good of the spouses and the procreation and education of children, it comes as no surprise that marriage does not apply to two homosexual parties. Moreover, the covenantal relationship between husband and wife is a mirror of the covenantal union between Christ as groom and the Church as bride. The legal union of a groom with a groom or a bride with a bride completely obliterations the biblical reflection of the union between Christ (male) and His Church (female).

Homosexual unions, by their very nature, fall outside the framework of this divine plan for marriage. Anatomically, the procreative organs of the male and female are ordered to one another for the procreation of children: "the two shall become one flesh." While all human persons are created in the image of God and possess inherent dignity, the act of homosexual intercourse is sinful according to Natural Law and Sacred Scripture.

Natural Law clearly reveals that marriage serves two primary purposes: the procreative purpose (the generation and upbringing of children) and the unitive purpose (the mutual love and support of the spouses). These purposes are inseparably linked, and when separated, the true meaning of marriage is diminished.

Homosexual relationships are not ordered to these ends. Unlike the union of a man and a woman, such relationships cannot result in the creation of new life. For this reason, same-sex unions are contrary to nature and cannot be considered equivalent to the covenant of marriage. The Greek philosopher Plato, basing his conclusion on Natural Law made this observation:

> "When male unites with male or female with female, contrary to nature, the offense is worthy of blame and punishment."[9]

As observed previously, the Christian should not limit himself to Natural Law, although it is sufficient on this matter. Jesus Christ affirms the original design for marriage: "Have you not read that from the beginning the Creator made them male and female"

(Matthew 19:4)? The Apostle Paul also addresses the immorality of homosexuality in his Epistle to the Romans, Paul describes same-sex acts as contrary to God's design and part of the fallen nature of humanity:

> Therefore, God gave them up to the desires of their heart, unto uncleanness: to dishonor their own bodies among themselves. Who changed the truth of God into a lie; and worshipped and served the creature rather than the Creator, who is blessed forever. Amen.
>
> For this cause, God delivered them up to shameful affections. For their women have changed the natural use into that use which is against nature. And, in like manner, the men also, leaving the natural use of the women, have burned in their lusts one towards another, men with men working that which is filthy, and receiving in themselves the recompense which was due to their error. And as they liked not to have God in their knowledge, God delivered them up to a reprobate sense, to do those things which are not convenient (Romans 1:24–28).

Some proponents of homosexuality wish to assert that the term "homosexual" never appears in the Bible and is not explicitly condemned. However, a knowledge of the original Greek terms dispels this false claim. The Apostle Paul twice condemns the act of *arsenokoitai* in 1 Corinthians 6:9 and 1 Timothy 1:10. The Greek word is a compound of *arsēn* (male) and *koitē* (bed, often implying sexual relations). The latter word, *koitē,* is etymologically related to the Latin word *coitus*—a euphemism for sexual intercourse. Translated literally, the sin of *arsenokoitai* is "men bedding of men." The Apostle Paul says:

> "Know you not that the unjust shall not possess the kingdom of God? Do not err: neither fornicators, nor idolaters, nor adulterers, nor the effeminate, *nor liers with mankind* (*arsenokoitai*), nor thieves, nor covetous, nor drunkards, nor railers, nor extortioners, shall possess the kingdom of God" (1 Corinthians 6:9).

Paul's list of sins includes fornication, idolatry, adultery, theft, drunkenness, and extortion. The Christian message is that all sins are forgivable and mercy is extended to all. The temptation toward homosexual acts does not exclude anyone from the mercy of God. All those who have committed any of these sins, or all those tempted to commit these sins are called to a life of faith, mercy, love, and repentance.

The redefinition of marriage to include homosexual marriage is not in accord with Natural Law or the Holy Bible. Nevertheless, Christians should reach out to those tempted to homosexuality with respect, compassion, and sensitivity. We should treat every person with love and kindness. Our Lord Jesus Christ invited everyone to enter the kingdom through repentance and faith. Our Christian worldview is rooted in the belief that God's plan for human sexuality leads to human flourishing and that deviating from this plan ultimately causes harm.

We are not insisting on a preferred belief about marriage. We are insisting on God's definition of marriage. Marriage is not a matter of personal opinion because it has implications for the broader society. Traditionally understood, marriage is the foundational unit of society. It provides the necessary context for nurturing and educating children and contributes to social stability and prosperity.

Christians rightly observe that such a redefinition could lead to confusion about the nature and purpose of marriage, weakening the institution as a whole. If the government can redefine God's definition of "marriage," why can't it redefine the definition of "male and female"? The laws of a nation must be based on observing Natural Law—not on the agenda of the New Secular Religion.

ACTION ITEMS FOR THE CHRISTIAN PATRIOT

1. Define Matrimony in accordance with Natural Law, Genesis, and the teaching of Jesus Christ:

   "MATRIMONY or MARRIAGE is the monogamous union of a biological man and biological woman having reached the age of majority. Marriage is rendered valid and binding when the man and woman make vows of their own free volition, without compulsion, to form a legal and spiritual covenant "until death do us part."

2. Overturn No-Fault Divorce as contrary to Natural Law, Genesis, and the teaching of Jesus Christ.
3. Overturn any legal redefinition of marriage to include homosexual unions.

STRATEGY 4

FAMILY AND BIRTHRATES

The social structures that protected and nurtured marriage and family have eroded, and the New Secular Religion has filled the vacuum left by Christians abandoning the public square. Consequently, we have seen a rapid decline in marriage rates and birth rates. In the 1950s, the marriage rate in the United States reached 92 percent. Since the 1950s, the erosion of Christian culture and the infiltration of secularism, "free-love," and no-fault divorce have wreaked havoc on our marriage rates. According to the US Census Bureau, the marriage rate fell to 72 percent in the 1960s and collapsed to about 51 percent in 2021.

It is not surprising that birth rates have also plummeted. The Total Fertility Rate (TFR) measures the birth rate in terms of the average number of children born per woman. Sociologists have historically observed that a TFR of 2.1 is required to maintain replacement levels. In the United States the TFR has crashed since the 1960s:

- For the first several decades of the 1900s, the TFR averaged about 3.5 children per woman.
- After World War II, the Baby Boom of the 1950s lifted the TFR to approximately 3.7 children per woman.

- The birth rate began to decline in the 1960s due to the availability of birth control, the sexual revolution, and society's embrace of feminism.
- By the 1970s, the TFR had dropped to about 2.0 children per woman, below the needed 2.1 replacement level.
- In the 1980s, the TFR fell slightly to 1.8–2.0 children per woman.
- In the 2010s, the TFR fell to 1.7–1.8 children per woman.
- In 2020, the TFR reached a historic low of about 1.64 children per woman.

You don't need a degree in sociology to see that the drop from a TFR of 3.5 to 1.64 aligns with the rise of the New Secular Religion. Traditional marriage is ridiculed in schools, universities, television programs, and films. Young people, especially women, are taught that careers are more significant than marriage and raising children. How did we arrive at this point?

BE FRUITFUL AND MULTIPLY?

We might feel inclined to shrug off these numbers. However, the TFR may be one of the most vital indicators of a culture's health. If a farmer experienced a 50 percent drop in crop yield, he would be devastated. The same applies to a cattle rancher or sheepherder noticing a 50 percent reduction in the fertility of his livestock. He would immediately begin investigating the environment. What caused this drastic change? Chemicals? Pollution? Disease? Insects? Drought? He rightfully would examine the factors contributing to the decline. A negative birth rate is cultural suicide, and the Christian Patriot must explore the environmental issues leading to demographic collapse.

Natural Law points to fecundity as a sign of health. We delight in observing flowering landscapes, flourishing bees, clean streams, and lakes teeming with fish, while wildlife frolics and ecosystems remain in harmony. We are part of that ecosystem, and our declining birthrate signals our eventual status as an endangered species. Ideological environmentalists, who fundamentally resent humanity, may celebrate the demographic collapse of birth rates. That is not the Christian perspective. God not only expects human fecundity; He also commands it.

> "And God created man to his own image: to the image of God he created him: male and female he created them. And God blessed them, saying: Increase and multiply, and fill the earth, and subdue it, and rule over the fishes of the sea, and the fowls of the air, and all living creatures that move upon the earth" (Genesis 1:27–28).
>
> "And God blessed Noah and his sons. And he said to them: Increase and multiply, and fill the earth" (Genesis 9:1).

Human fecundity, however, is not simply dependent on human procreation. Humans have intellect and free will and adjust to their environments. Currently, the birth rate reveals an adjustment contrary to procreation—below replacement levels. Just as a farmer or rancher would examine the environmental factors affecting fecundity, as responsible patriots, we must also examine our cultural factors and enact policies that protect and promote the formation of marriages and families for the good of society.

ECONOMIC AND POLITICAL SECURITY FOR FAMILIES

The post-WWII economic boom led to a period of affluence and optimism in the 1950s. This led to what is now called the baby boom, when marriage and childbearing were viewed as central to the American Dream. The availability of jobs, increased prosperity, and a focus on family life during this period created conditions in which many people married young and had multiple children. Economic security was seen as a prerequisite for starting a family, and during the 1950s, having children became associated with social status and a strong, stable society.

The 1960s challenged this consensus with the introduction of contraception, abortion, and no-fault divorce. The natural connection between marriage, sex, and family was dismantled. The emergence of feminism also coincided with this time because women were able to have sexual intercourse *while* preventing pregnancy and birth. This set the stage for promiscuous sexual activity without the risk of pregnancy. The decade of free love and hippies was the result of birth control and access to abortion.

There were also economic factors. In 1971, President Richard Nixon ended the Bretton Woods System that backed the value of the US dollar to gold. The immediate result (still felt today) was an atmospheric increase in inflation. Savings were devalued, debt was encouraged, and the price of homes increased at a rate greater than annual income. This economic change worked against the traditional ideal of marriage, the father as a single-income provider, and the raising of children. The inflationary economy made traditional family life less feasible. To keep up, more women had entered the workforce, making the traditional stay-at-home-mother model less financially viable for many families. The introduction of no-fault divorce in the 1970s and 1980s also paved the way for broken families. By the 1970s, divorce reached the level of one in three marriages ending in divorce. In the 1980s, the divorce rate peaked to one in two marriages ending in divorce. The children raised within this new landscape of divorce naturally avoided marriage as they entered adulthood.

Culturally, the feminist movement, which gained momentum in the 1960s and 1970s, emphasized gender equality and women's rights, particularly in areas like education, career opportunities, and reproductive rights. Under the influence of the secularized culture, young women increasingly joined the workforce, often delaying marriage and childbirth as they focused on their career paths. Feminism also helped break down traditional gender roles that emphasized the importance of women as primarily wives and mothers, allowing women to prioritize corporate status and wage earning.

In the 1970s and 1980s, cohabitation (living together without marriage) became more widely accepted. Many couples began living together before marriage, or without marrying at all, due to shifting views about the necessity of marriage. This is particularly evident in younger generations, who increasingly see marriage as optional or unnecessary. The traditional Christian custom to marry young and have children began to fade, and the increasing acceptance of divorce allowed for greater flexibility in how people approached marriage as a "contract" rather than as a "covenant." Consequently, the median age at first marriage for men reached twenty-nine, and, for women, it reached twenty-seven by the 2010s.

THE FOURTEEN BENEFITS OF TRADITIONAL FAMILIES

Birthrates show us the trend, but family is not merely the data points of birthrates on a graph. God's will is not our will, and the number of children is limited or expanded by the unseen providence of God. The goal is not merely to "pump those numbers" but to create happy and holy families where marriage thrives and children develop within the safety of a loving home.

Nothing can replace the virtue and goodwill of a happily married couple raising children in the best way they know how. Nevertheless, families are boosted and assisted by protection, laws, and tax policies that aid and assist those families that are shouldering the burden of building the next generation of citizens and patriots. The Christian Patriot must advocate for policies that nurture and enrich the economic and legal place of families as the building blocks of a healthy society.

Study after study confirms that children raised in traditional families with happily married parents fare better than those who do not have this advantage. Our aim is not to shame or criticize parents raising children in non-traditional settings, but rather to promote a culture that enables more children to grow up in the best possible circumstances. Children in traditional two-parent households typically benefit from a range of advantages that can positively impact their emotional, social, academic, and economic development. While many single-parent households provide excellent care and support, research consistently indicates that children in two-parent homes often have access to benefits that can enhance their overall well-being. Here are some key advantages of two-parent households:

1. **Parental Support and Emotional Regulation:** Children in two-parent households often have more consistent access to emotional support, which can help them manage stress, frustration, and anxiety. Having both parents available allows for more balanced emotional nurturing, as each parent may bring different strengths in terms of empathy, discipline, and emotional guidance.

2. **Security and Stability:** Two-parent households often provide greater emotional security, as children have the opportunity to form strong relationships with both parents, which can help build a stronger sense of stability and resilience.
3. **Financial Security:** One of the primary advantages of two-parent households is the potential for income. Traditional families tend to have higher income due to stability. Divorce is shown to greatly reduce the wealth of families and individuals. Moreover, singleparents naturally struggle due to the increased stress of balancing employment and childcare.
4. **Economic Mobility:** Studies have shown that children in two-parent households generally experience better economic outcomes as they grow older due to more financial resources, better access to educational opportunities, and the ability to accumulate wealth over time.
5. **Higher Educational Attainment:** Research consistently finds that children in two-parent households tend to perform better academically. Two-parent families often have more time and resources to devote to their children's education, which can include helping with homework, attending parent-teacher conferences, and supporting academic enrichment programs.
6. **Positive Role Models:** With both parents involved, children have access to more role models who may encourage them to value education and work hard to achieve academic success. Fathers, in particular, are shown to have a positive influence on academic achievement when they are actively involved in their children's education.

7. **Social Skills and Peer Relationships:** Children in two-parent households often have more opportunities to learn appropriate social behaviors from both parents. A two-parent family offers diverse social interactions and communication models, helping children learn how to navigate relationships with peers and authority figures.
8. **Reduced Risk of Delinquency:** Studies have shown that children raised in two-parent households are generally less likely to engage in delinquent behavior or encounter trouble with the law compared with those raised in single-parent households. The presence of two parents is associated with more consistent supervision and discipline, which can reduce risky behaviors.
9. **Balanced Views on Gender Roles:** In two-parent households, children are exposed to different gender roles as modeled by both a mother and a father. This can provide them with a more balanced understanding of gender dynamics and responsibilities, which can help them develop healthier relationships as they grow up.
10. **Health Benefits:** Children in two-parent households tend to have better physical and mental health outcomes. This may be due in part to the increased financial resources available for healthcare, better access to nutritious food, and the stability of living in a well-supported environment. Additionally, research has shown that the involvement of both parents can help promote a child's physical well-being by encouraging healthier lifestyles and regular check-ups.
11. **Access to Enrichment:** With two parents involved, children often have more opportunities to participate in extracurricular activities like sports, arts, and clubs. These activities help children develop well-rounded skills, build self-esteem,

and explore their interests. In many cases, two-parent households are more likely to be able to afford these opportunities and transport children to and from events.

12. **Healthy Relationships:** In two-parent households, children have the opportunity to observe how two adults interact, negotiate, and resolve conflicts within the context of a committed partnership. Healthy communication, mutual respect, and conflict resolution skills modeled by parents can have a significant impact on a child's understanding of relationships, and influence their future relationships as adults.
13. **More Decision-Making Support:** Two-parent households allow for a collaborative approach to decision-making when it comes to raising children. This can result in more thoughtful, well-rounded decisions regarding education, discipline, and overall child-rearing. The input of two parents can help ensure a balance of perspectives and needs are considered.
14. **Stronger Social Cohesion:** Two-parent households are often seen as a foundational building block of stable communities. Families that have strong support systems tend to contribute positively to societal cohesion. Children raised in stable two-parent families are more likely to grow up with values that emphasize community, responsibility, and respect for others.

While many children from single-parent households thrive and find success, the overall evidence suggests that children from two-parent households often experience certain benefits related to emotional well-being, financial stability, academic performance, and socialization. The involvement of both parents provides additional support, role models, and resources that can enhance the overall development of a child. However, it's important to acknowledge that individual circumstances and the quality of relationships matter significantly, and a healthy, supportive environment—whether in a two-parent or single-parent household—is the key to a child's well-being.

HOW DO WE ENCOURAGE TRADITIONAL FAMILIES?

Contemporary nations are now identifying the benefit of promoting traditional families through policies. Hungary, in particular, has been a pioneer in using direct financial incentives to encourage intact marriages, family success, and safer homes for children. Under the leadership of Prime Minister Viktor Orbán, Hungary has implemented several pro-family policies with proven results.

Hungarian Family Strategy

1. **Family Tax Benefits:** Hungary introduced a family tax system that provides substantial tax relief for families with children. Families receive tax breaks based on the number of children they have, and larger families benefit from significant tax reductions. For instance, in 2020, families with three or more children could claim over 200,000 forints (about $660) per child in tax reductions.
2. **Housing and Loan Benefits:** The government also introduced a program called the CSOK, which provides subsidized housing loans to families with children. This initiative has made it easier for families to buy homes, particularly for young couples who are just starting out. In addition to housing benefits, Hungary has implemented a subsidized car purchase program for families with children designed to help reduce transportation costs.

3. **Support for Stay-at-Home Mothers:** Hungary has also introduced programs to support stay-at-home mothers, including policies that ensure mothers can continue to receive benefits such as health insurance and pensions while they care for their children at home.

Sweden has also recognized the social benefits of assisting families and has experimented with helpful initiatives, such as:

Swedish Family Strategy

1. **Child Allowance and Tax Breaks:** The Swedish government provides a monthly child allowance for families, which is available for every child under the age of sixteen. This allowance helps offset some of the costs of raising children. Furthermore, the Swedish tax system is progressive, with parents benefiting from reduced taxes based on family size, making it more financially attractive for couples to have more children.
2. **Generous Parental Leave:** Sweden offers one of the most generous parental leave systems in the world, with 480 days of paid leave per child. The leave can be divided between the parents as they see fit, allowing for flexibility and greater involvement of fathers in child-rearing. A significant portion of this leave is reserved for fathers, ensuring that men participate equally in caring for their children.

France has also recently implemented policies to boost families:

French Family Strategy

1. **Pro-Family Tax Incentives:** France offers a family-based tax system known as the "quotient familial" system. Under this system, families receive tax benefits based on the num-

ber of children they have. The more children a family has, the lower the overall tax burden. This system is designed to make it financially easier for families to support multiple children. Parents with children may receive tax reductions that increase as the number of children in the household grows.

2. **Family Allowances:** In 1939, France started providing direct payments to families with children.
3. **Parental Leave and Childcare Support:** France also provides generous parental leave policies. Mothers are entitled to sixteen weeks of paid maternity leave, while fathers can take up to twenty-eight days of paternity leave.

To summarize these various initiatives, we observe the following:

1. **Tax Breaks and Child Credits:** If a married couple files jointly, they receive tax benefits. There is a system of graduated tax reduction based on the number of children being raised in the home. This takes the form both of reductions in taxes and/or the direct award of credit based on the number of children at home.
2. **Allowances:** In France, each family is given a monthly allowance to offset the expense of raising a child. Singapore currently sponsors lump-sum payments for each child born.
3. **Housing and Loan Benefits:** The government gives loans to families, similar to subsidized and sponsored loans for veterans.
4. **Travel Benefits:** The government gives discounts or tax reductions for purchasing vehicles needed for children, such as minivans or SUVs.
5. **Parental Leave:** Countries promote parental leave for the birth of a child.

6. **Subsidies for Stay-at-Home Mothers:** In Hungary, subsidies are granted to promote the presence of mothers in the home caring for children.
7. **Birth Coverage:** Scandalously, government and corporate systems have covered abortion, but not the live birth of citizens. The cost of delivery for the birth of a citizen could easily be covered by the government.

To those who might object to these suggestions, keep in mind that the government already rewards veterans, immigrants, convicts, special interest groups, and foreigners on work and student visas with generous subsidies. It is not that this is not already being done *for some people*. We must ask ourselves, who receives priority? Surely, our families and our veterans should come to the front of the line. Raising virtuous, healthy, and strong children is one of the most important tasks for building a strong and noble nation.

ACTION ITEMS

1. Recognize that a birthrate under 2.1 is unhealthy and reveals spiritual and cultural decline.
2. Teach the biblical principle that children are a blessing and that large families are a delight.
3. Teach that the traditional family is not only sanctioned by God, but also that it carries fourteen tangible benefits for the children.
4. Create financial incentives and tax breaks for married couples seeking to grow their family.

STRATEGY 5

END ABORTION WITH COMPASSION AND CONVICTION

For Christians, the sanctity of human life is a cornerstone of faith, rooted in the belief that every person is created in God's image. Abortion—the deliberate termination of a preborn child's life—stands in stark opposition to this biblical truth, constituting a grave sin. The Bible provides a consistent testimony to the value of life from conception and explicitly condemns the shedding of innocent blood. The Old and New Testaments, along with early Christian writers, echo this, explicitly denouncing abortion as a violation of God's law. Through Scripture and Natural Law, Christians find a unified call to protect the unborn, revealing abortion as an affront to the Creator's design. With the legalization of abortion and the cultural shift away from God and chastity, abortion (and the scars it leaves) has become increasingly widespread. A reasonable current estimate is that between 14 percent and 25 percent of American women have had an abortion, with the higher end, closer to 25 percent, being most likely.[1]

SANCTITY OF LIFE IN SCRIPTURE

The Bible establishes human life as sacred, beginning with its origin in God's creative act. Genesis 1:27 declares, "And God created man to his own image: to the image of God he created him: male and female he created them." This divine imprint endows every human with intrinsic worth, a truth that extends to the preborn. Psalm 138:13–14 affirms God's intimate involvement in forming life: "For you formed my inward parts; you knitted me together in my mother's womb. I praise you, for I am fearfully and wonderfully made. Wonderful are your works; my soul knows it very well."[2] Here, David acknowledges that God knows and shapes us even before birth, marking the womb as a sanctuary of divine craftsmanship.

God, through Moses, commands, "Thou shalt not kill" (Exodus 20:13), a prohibition against taking innocent life. The preborn, defenseless, and faultless epitomize innocence. Proverbs 6:16–17 lists among God's hatreds "hands that shed innocent blood," a sin abortion directly commits. Jeremiah 1:5 further reveals God's pre-birth purpose: "Before I formed thee in the womb of thy mother, I knew thee: and before thou camest forth out of the womb, I sanctified thee, and made thee a prophet unto the nations." The unborn Jeremiah was known and consecrated, underscoring that life's value precedes birth.

Luke 1:41–44 offers a New Testament witness: "And it came to pass, that when Elizabeth heard the salutation of Mary, the infant leaped in her womb.... And she cried out with a loud voice, and said: Blessed art thou among women, and blessed is the fruit of thy womb." John the Baptist, yet unborn, responds to Christ's presence, affirming the personhood of the preborn. Abortion, by ending such lives, defies God's sacred order.

SIN AND THE SHEDDING OF BLOOD

Abortion's sinfulness lies not only in its violation of life's sanctity but in its nature as murder. The Bible consistently condemns bloodshed, especially of the innocent. Genesis 9:6 states, "Whosoever shall shed man's blood, his blood shall be shed: for man was made to the image of God." This penalty reflects the gravity of destroying a life bearing God's likeness, a principle applicable to the unborn. Job 10:8–11 marvels at prenatal creation: "Thy hands have made me, and fashioned me wholly round about.... Hast thou not poured me out as milk, and curdled me like cheese?" To abort is to unravel God's handiwork, an act of rebellion against the Creator.

The New Testament deepens this ethic. Our Lord Jesus Christ reiterates, "You shall not murder" (Matthew 19:18). Abortion, far from loving one's neighbor, destroys the most vulnerable. Scripture also condemns those who enable evil. Christians who fail to protect the innocent and unborn *share* in its guilt, making this sin a communal call to repentance and action.

EARLY CHRISTIAN CONDEMNATION OF ABORTION

The early Church, steeped in Scripture, unequivocally rejected abortion, viewing it as a continuation of pagan immorality. The *Didache*, a first-century Christian manual, commands, "Thou shalt not murder a child by abortion nor kill that which is begotten." This explicit prohibition links abortion to murder, reflecting the Church's understanding of Exodus 20:13 and the unborn baby's personhood. Written within decades of the apostles, the *Didache* reveals that the grave sinfulness of abortion was a settled matter from the time of the apostles.

The Apocalypse of Peter, an early pseudonymous Christian text dating from AD 90–150, contains the second oldest reference to abortion in Christian literature, framing it as a grave sin with vivid consequences in the afterlife. This work, written in the form of a vision revealed to the Apostle Peter by the risen Jesus, describes the punishments awaiting various sinners in hell. Among these, it specifically addresses unrepentant women who have aborted their children as they suffer in the sight of their children:

> And near that place I saw another strait place into which the gore and the filth of those who were being punished ran down and became there as it were a lake: and there sat women having the gore up to their necks, and over against them sat many children who were born to them out of due time, crying; and there came forth from them sparks of fire and smote the women in the eyes: and these were the accursed who conceived and caused abortion.[3]

Notably, these women suffering in hell did not repent and turn to Christ. Forgiveness is always offered by Jesus Christ.

Tertullian, a second-century Christian, elaborates in *Apology* (Chapter 9): "To hinder a birth is merely a speedier man-killing; nor does it matter whether you take away a life that is born, or destroy one that is coming to the birth." Tertullian ties abortion to the image of God, arguing that the unborn infant, though not yet fully formed, possesses the full potential of humanity—a potential God alone may govern.

Athenagoras, in his *Plea for the Christians* (ca. AD 177), defends Christians against false charges, stating, "We say that those women who use drugs to bring on abortion commit murder, and they will have to give an account to God." This reflects a consensus: abortion was not merely sinful but a grave offense requiring divine judgment. These early Christian writings, echoing Scripture, affirm that abortion violates God's law, a stance unbroken in orthodox Christian tradition.

Abortion is sinful because it contradicts the Bible's testimony to life's sanctity and the early Church's unwavering rejection of it. Genesis 1:27 and Psalm 138:13–14 reveal the unborn as God's image-bearers, crafted with purpose. Exodus 20:13 and Proverbs 6:17 condemn their destruction as murder, a sin magnified by their innocence. Luke 1:41–44 and Jeremiah 1:5 affirm their personhood, while Romans 13:9 and 1 John 3:15 frame abortion as a failure of love. Early Christians, from the *Didache*'s blunt command to Tertullian's theological clarity, saw abortion as an abomination, rooted in Scripture's ethic. For modern Christians, this heritage demands a clear stance: abortion is not a mere moral failing but a profound sin against God's creative will. To uphold the Gospel of life is to defend the preborn, reflecting Christ's love for the least among us.

THE GUILT OF ABORTION

For any woman who has sought an abortion—and for those who have enabled or promoted abortion—the weight of guilt, shame, or sorrow can feel unbearable. The devil whispers that you've crossed a line too far for redemption. Yet, from a Christian perspective, this is not the end of your story. The Gospel of Jesus Christ proclaims a truth more powerful than any sin: forgiveness is offered through Christ's boundless love and mercy. No matter what you've done, Christ's arms remain open, ready to heal and restore a heart broken in repentance.

The Bible assures us that God's mercy surpasses human failing. David cries, "Have mercy on me, O God, according to thy great mercy. And according to the multitude of thy tender mercies blot out my iniquity." David, a man who sinned gravely (adultery and arranging a murder), found forgiveness when he turned to God with a contrite heart. Your abortion does not make you an exception; it makes you a candidate for that same mercy. Romans 5:20 declares, "But where sin abounded, grace did more abound." Christ's sacrifice on the cross was not limited—it covers every sin, including yours, when you seek Him.

Consider the woman caught in adultery in John 8:10–11: "Then Jesus lifting up himself, said to her: Woman, where are they that accused thee? Hath no man condemned thee? She said: No man, Lord. And Jesus said: Neither will I condemn thee. Go, and now sin no more." Jesus did not define her by her past, but rather offered her a new beginning. He offers us the same. 1 John 1:9 promises, "If we confess our sins, he is faithful and just, to forgive us our sins, and to cleanse us from all iniquity." Confession, whether in prayer or sacrament, opens the door to this cleansing grace.

The early Church understood this, too. Saint Augustine, once steeped in sin himself, wrote in *Confessions* (Book IX), "Thou hast made us for Thyself, O Lord, and our heart is restless until it rests in Thee." Your restlessness—your guilt—can find peace in Christ. Modern ministries like Rachel's Vineyard, rooted in Christian compassion, echo this, offering retreats where women process their grief and encounter God's love. You are not alone; countless women have walked this road and found healing.

You may fear God's judgment, but Scripture sings of His love instead. Isaiah 1:18 invites, "If your sins be as scarlet, they shall be made as white as snow." Bring your pain to Jesus—He bore it on the cross. You are not forsaken; you are forgiven. Step into His light, dear sister, and let His mercy rewrite your story with hope.

ENDING ABORTION PRACTICALLY AND POLITICALLY

Abortion stands as a stark moral and cultural challenge in the United States. The nation remains deeply divided, even after the 2022 *Dobbs v. Jackson Women's Health Organization* decision overturned *Roe v. Wade*, shifting abortion regulation to the states. The Guttmacher Institute estimates over 600,000 abortions occur annually, driven by economic pressures, lack of support, and a permissive legal framework in many regions. For American Christians, whose faith traditions affirm life's sanctity from conception, this reality demands a response that is both practical and principled. The Catholic Church, rooted in teachings like the Catechism's assertion that "human life must be respected and protected absolutely from the moment of conception" (*Catechism of the Catholic Church* 2270), and evangelical Christians, mobilized since the 1970s, share a common call: to end abortion. Yet, prohibition alone is insufficient. To truly abolish abortion, the faithful must address its root causes—ending the need—while dismantling its legal scaffolding through political activism, executive action, and defunding organizations like Planned Parenthood.

Christian Patriot offers a dual strategy. First, it explores how Christians can reduce abortion demand through compassionate support for women and families. Second, it outlines a roadmap to make abortion illegal nationwide, leveraging political mobilization, judicial influence, and executive power. Finally, it addresses defunding Planned Parenthood and other pro-death NGOs that serve as linchpins in the Big Abortion lobby. By appealing to both mercy and justice, the faithful can transform their cities, states, and nations into places where abortion is neither sought nor sanctioned—a culture of life where every child is welcomed and every mother is upheld.

ENDING THE DEMAND FOR ABORTION

The persistence of abortion is tied to desperation. Economic insecurity, inadequate healthcare, and lack of familial or community support drive many women to abortion clinics. A 2023 Guttmacher study found that 75 percent of abortion patients cited financial hardship or an inability to care for a child as primary reasons for an abortion. For Christians, this is a call to action—not just to condemn, but to console and provide. Ending the demand for abortion begins with addressing these root causes through faith-driven compassion.

Crisis pregnancy centers (CPCs), numbering over 2,500 nationwide according to Heartbeat International, offer free ultrasounds, counseling, and material aid—diapers, formula, and clothing—to women in crisis.[4] Organizations like the Gabriel Network provide housing and mentorship for pregnant mothers, while Catholic Charities supports thousands annually with food, medical care, and job training. Adoption advocacy is another pillar: evangelical ministries like Bethany Christian Services facilitate thousands of adoptions yearly, presenting a life-affirming alternative. These efforts embody Christ's command to love the least among us, reducing abortion rates by meeting tangible needs.

Beyond direct aid, Christians can advocate for policies that ease motherhood's burdens. Paid family leave, currently unavailable to 73 percent of US workers per the Bureau of Labor Statistics, could be a bipartisan cause, with faith leaders lobbying state and federal lawmakers.[5] Affordable childcare and expanded Medicaid coverage for prenatal and postnatal care—already championed by pro-life governors like Ron DeSantis in Florida—further lighten the load. Culturally, churches can shift attitudes by celebrating motherhood and fatherhood, countering secular narratives that frame children as obstacles. This approach aligns with the sanctity of life ethic.

By building a support network so robust that abortion becomes unthinkable, Christians and Catholics can erode its demand, paving the way for its legal end.

POLITICAL ACTIVISM TO BAN ABORTION

Making abortion illegal in all fifty states requires political muscle, and Christians—especially Evangelicals and Catholics—wield significant influence. Since the Moral Majority's rise in the 1970s, the religious Right has reshaped the Republican Party, securing pro-life planks in its platform. Post-Dobbs, fourteen states have enacted near-total abortion bans, with others like Texas and Oklahoma using "heartbeat" laws to restrict access. Yet, blue states like California and New York enshrine abortion rights, necessitating a national strategy.

Grassroots activism is key. Churches, with over 60 million regular attendees per Gallup polls, can mobilize voters, host candidate forums, and lobby legislators.[6] Nationally, electing pro-life presidents and senators ensures a pipeline of conservative judges and policies. The 2024 election, potentially amplifying Trump-era gains, could solidify this momentum if Christians prioritize single-issue voting.

State-level successes offer a blueprint. Trigger laws, pre-written to activate post-Roe, banned abortion in states like Tennessee within months. Heartbeat bills, detecting fetal cardiac activity at six weeks, have curbed abortions in Georgia and Ohio. Federal action, though, is the ultimate goal—a Human Life Amendment or national ban—requiring a pro-life Congress and White House. Historical precedent exists: the 1980s saw Reagan align Evangelicals and Catholics into a voting bloc that persists today.

Unity is critical. Despite theological differences, Catholics and Evangelical Protestants share this cause. The US Conference of

Catholic Bishops and groups like Focus on the Family can coordinate campaigns, amplifying impact. Political activism, fueled by faith, can close the gaps Dobbs left open, ensuring abortion's illegality coast to coast.

COURTS AND EXECUTIVE ORDERS

The judiciary and executive branches are pivotal in ending abortion legally. Courts set precedents; executives enforce them. Dobbs, overturning Roe with a 6–3 Supreme Court majority bolstered by Trump appointees Gorsuch, Kavanaugh, and Barrett, proved judicial appointments' power. Christians must sustain this by electing presidents who nominate originalist justices and senators who confirm them. Future cases—like challenges to late-term abortion or interstate abortion travel—could further restrict access, potentially banning it outright if the Court deems fetuses persons under the 14th Amendment.

State courts matter too. In states like Kansas, where a 2019 ruling found abortion in the state constitution, pro-life groups must back judicial candidates to reverse such precedents. Legal advocacy groups like the Alliance Defending Freedom and Thomas More Society play a role, filing suits that climb to federal courts, testing limits post-Dobbs.

Executive action complements this. Presidents can issue orders like the Mexico City Policy, which was reinstated by Trump in 2017, barring foreign aid to abortion-promoting NGOs. Domestically, the 2019 Protect Life Rule under Title X cut Planned Parenthood's federal funding by $60 million, redirecting it to non-abortion providers. A pro-life administration could expand this, using the Department of Health and Human Services (HHS) to tighten regulations or the Department of Justice to prosecute abortion law violations in ban states. Executive orders, while temporary, signal intent and shift resources—critical steps toward a national ban.

DEFUNDING PLANNED PARENTHOOD

Planned Parenthood, performing over 390,000 abortions annually per its 2023 report, is a cornerstone of abortion's infrastructure.[7] It receives roughly $670 million yearly in public funds, mostly via Medicaid and Title X. Defunding it is both symbolic and strategic, stripping resources from the nation's largest abortion provider.

Legislative efforts have faltered—2017's ACA repeal attempt to defund Planned Parenthood failed by one Senate vote—but Dobbs renews the push. States like Texas and Missouri have excluded Planned Parenthood from Medicaid, redirecting funds to Federally Qualified Health Centers (FQHCs), which offer comprehensive care without abortions. Nationally, a Republican Congress could pass budget riders, barring abortion providers from federal dollars, a tactic that was nearly successful in 2021. Christians can pressure lawmakers, with groups like Susan B. Anthony Pro-Life America, which targets swing districts.

Opponents argue this harms women's healthcare, but FQHCs outnumber Planned Parenthood clinics twenty-to-one, serving millions without abortion ties. Defunding simply prioritizes life-affirming care. Public campaigns—podcasts, door-knocking rallies, social media, church petitions—can counter Planned Parenthood's narrative, emphasizing its abortion focus over broader services.

CONCLUSION

Ending abortion demands a two-pronged assault: compassion to end its need and conviction to end its legality. Christian Patriots can lead by expanding support for mothers—through CPCs, policy advocacy, and cultural renewal—while wielding political power to ban abortion nationwide. Courts and executive orders amplify this, with defunding Planned Parenthood as a decisive blow. The faithful have the tools: a moral mandate, organizational strength, and a voting bloc that shapes elections.

The vision is a post-abortion America—a culture of life where economic security and community embrace replace abortion's allure, and laws reflect the dignity of every human soul. It requires unity, perseverance, and faith. As St. John Paul II wrote in *Evangelium Vitae*, "The Gospel of life is at the heart of Jesus' message." By living that Gospel, American Christians can forge a nation where abortion is a relic of the past, replaced by justice, mercy, and love for both mother and child.

ACTION ITEMS

1. Theologically educate Christians and the public to believe that the Bible and Natural Law are opposed to abortion.
2. Preach forgiveness and repentance for those who have committed abortion or facilitated the sin.
3. Support and fund crisis pregnancy centers that provide sonograms, counseling, and care for at-risk mothers.
4. Seek political activation through social campaigns and elections to place leaders who will work to overturn protections for abortion.
5. Defund the NGOs that promote, fund, and extend abortion globally.

STRATEGY 6

SCHOOL CHOICE AND HOMESCHOOL

"Train up a child in the way he should go, and when he is old, he will not depart from it."

—Proverbs 22:6

The duty and obligation of parents is the procreation and proper education of offspring rooted in Natural Law and the divine order. Saint Thomas Aquinas observed, "The procreation of children is the principal end of marriage; it is through this union that nature is perfected and society is perpetuated."[1] However, he also argued that bringing children into the world is insufficient without ensuring they are properly raised and educated, particularly in virtue and faith: "The education of children is necessary for their growth in virtue, which is essential for their development as rational creatures."[2]

Unlike horses and cattle that begin walking within hours of birth, human children grow, develop, and mature at a much slower pace. Saint Thomas Aquinas observed, "Human offspring require long-term care and instruction. Thus, the union of man and woman in marriage is ordained for the common good, primarily the nurturing and education of children."[3]

As human persons, we are ordered not merely to family, work, faith, love, and virtue in this life. God also draws us toward a supernatural end of eternal beatitude in heaven through Jesus Christ. Education is the means by which this is passed down from one generation to the next.

> *"And these words which I command thee*
> *this day, shall be in thy heart:*
> *and thou shalt teach them diligently to thy children."*
>
> —Deuteronomy 6:6–7

Education derives from the Latin word *educare,* meaning "to lead out or draw out." Plato rightly taught: "Education is not the filling of a vessel, but the turning of the soul toward the light."[4] Aristotle also said, "The cultivation of virtue must be the goal of education, for it is by virtue that a person becomes good and fulfills his purpose."[5]

Education has long been a vital concern for Christians. From the earliest days of the Church, followers of Christ have sought to educate their children in both the wisdom of the world and the knowledge of God. Saint Augustine stated, "The purpose of learning is to discover truth, and that truth is ultimately found in God."[6]

The New Secular Religion has perverted the purpose of education. Education is a government apparatus of indoctrination. They are not "turning children to the light" (Plato) or showing "truth is ultimately found in God" (Augustine), but seeking to corrupt young minds with atheism, doubt, rebellion, Marxism, and cynicism. Schools are plagued with the idols of the New Secular Religion: BLM slogans, icons of Che Guevara, and LGBTQ+ flags. They push the dogmas of DEI, Critical Race Theory, and gender ideology, while test scores in reading, mathematics, geography, and history plummet. We are told "Keep your religion out of the schools," while they enforce strict dogma over the hearts and minds of impressionable young people.

Children are forced into guilt and victim narratives, leading to students being labeled as oppressors or victims based solely on their race. For example, the 1619 Project, which reinterprets American history by centering it around the legacy of slavery, has sparked significant debate. Critics say it promotes a biased and negative view of American history and promotes false guilt in white students. DEI agendas among school boards promote a shift from equality (equal opportunity) to equity (equal outcomes). The DEI idol of "Equity" has led to policies that favor certain groups at the expense of others while minimizing grades, effort, ranking, and outcomes for college acceptance and scholarships for students who try harder but are set back for the sake of "equal outcomes."

The Christian commitment to education dates back to the early Church, which established schools to provide both religious instruction and secular learning. During the Middle Ages, monasteries served as centers of learning, preserving classical texts and teaching a wide range of subjects. Later, universities such as Oxford, Cambridge, and the Sorbonne were founded with Christian principles at their core.

Gutenberg's invention of the printing press enabled the proliferation of books and the possibility of popular literacy and education. This allowed the Holy Bible to be printed and distributed freely. Soon, the Bible became the primer by which populations learned to read. Even as late as 1960, 42 percent of public school districts nationwide allowed or required Bible reading, and 50 percent reported some form of homeroom daily devotional prayer.[7] Since the 1960s, American public education has shifted away from its Christian foundations. In 1962, the US Supreme Court ruled in *Engel v. Vitale* that school-sponsored prayer was unconstitutional. The following year, in *Abington School District v. Schempp,* Bible reading in public schools was banned. These reversals contradicted the lived experience of Christians for centuries, and certainly that of Christian Americans since 1776. The New Secular Religion insisted on "separation of church and state" and, once separated, they invaded the empty space with their own godless cult of vice, Marxism, and degeneracy.

For many Christians in the 1960s, these landmark decisions marked a turning point in the decline of moral and spiritual values in education. They watched as the New Secular Religion pushed secular humanist philosophies into public school curricula, emphasizing relativism, downplaying logic, ignoring virtue, and rejecting absolute moral truths. This shift led Christian parents to seek alternatives that would reinforce their faith and values rather than undermine them. Two options emerged in the 1960s: private Christian schools and homeschooling.

PRIVATE CHRISTIAN SCHOOLS

Christian private schools flourished after the secularization of the public school system. Catholics had already pioneered an extensive network of private parochial schools since the 17th century as an alternative to secular public education. With the secularization of public schools, Protestants soon joined their ranks. Christian private schools freed parents and teachers to educate students academically, spiritually, and morally, preparing them for both worldly success and for faith in Christ.

Christian schools rightly prioritize academic rigor, believing that excellence in education honors God. Beginning in the 1980s—Christians took a renewed interest in classical education and the great books of Western civilization. This renewal promoted the conviction that education is not merely for employment but for the sake of truth itself. Christian students resurrected not only biblical literacy but also rediscovered the great classical texts of Homer, Plato, Aristotle, the Stoics, Virgil, the Church Fathers, Thomas Aquinas, Dante, and Cervantes.

Christian schools now have the freedom to introduce Christian prayer, catechism, worship, and spiritual direction on campus. Beyond academics, Christian schools can focus on character development, community service, and acts of charity as part of their curriculum.

HOMESCHOOL

Homeschooling was, in fact, the norm before the establishment of formal public schools. In colonial America, children were usually educated at home by their parents or tutors, especially in rural areas. Religious instruction was central to early home education and often supplemented by Sunday school or catechism classes at the local church by clergy.

The modern homeschool movement started in the 1960s and 1970s as part of two distinct ideological streams. Progressive educators (led by thinkers like John Holt) advocated for homeschooling as a way to escape rigid, authoritarian school systems and promote self-directed learning. Christian conservatives saw homeschooling as a means to provide a Christian education and protect children from secular influences in public schools. Christian parents chose homeschooling for a combination of reasons:

1. It is the biblical and traditional teaching (as expressed above by Thomas Aquinas) that the obligation to educate one's children belongs to the child's parents. The parent may del-

egate or supplement the child's education to a teacher or tutor (in loco parentis), but the parent remains the chief educator of her child.

2. The home is the most natural and convenient place of education, especially if the family pursues commerce from home, such as farming or homesteading.
3. Homeschooling allows for personalized, custom education experienced based on each child's learning style and interests.
4. Homeschooling saves time and avoids busywork.
5. Homeschooling allows for travel and removes the restraints of summer/winter breaks and semester restrictions.
6. Many Christian families homeschool to ensure their children receive an education consistent with their faith and values.
7. Christian private schools are often expensive, charging as much as $10,000 per child. Poor families or large families with four or more children cannot afford private tuition.

Christians who place their children in private Christian schools are often aligned with Christians who homeschool, and the communities often cross-pollinate with one another. Naturally, they are united in favor of the School Choice Movement.

THE SCHOOL CHOICE MOVEMENT

In recent decades, the School Choice Movement has gained momentum as a way to give parents greater control over their children's education. School choice policies allow public funding to follow the student, enabling families to choose the best educational option for their needs—whether that's a public school, private school, charter school, or homeschool.

Christians should vehemently oppose the monopoly of public education as now co-opted by the New Secular Religion. For Christian families, school choice is about more than academic quality; it's about the freedom to educate their children in accordance with their Christian beliefs. Secularists oppose School Choice because they perceive it as a threat to their government funding. The New Secular Religion covets your tax money and demands that they alone be granted the funding to push their dogmas and degeneracy on *your* children.

Christians *must* unite and fight for a generous policy of School Choice. In many states, the amount spent in public schools per student is $12,000.[8] With that in mind, here is a proposed plan for public policy and funding for School Choice:

1. The amount of $12,000 could be transferred as a voucher or coupon to a family for the sake of qualified homeschool education expenses, such as books, curriculum, and field trips. Imagine what a family of four children could accomplish with $48,000 for education annually.
2. The amount of $12,000 could be transferred as a voucher or coupon to pay for completely or offset the tuition of a private school.
3. Alternatively, if a voucher or coupon is not granted, a state could calculate the number of children by the amount of $12,000 and offset or cancel any income or property taxes owed by the family for the benefit of educating the children. This proposal is less attractive since poorer families who have less income or property would not receive enough money to purchase curriculum or pay the tuition at a private school.

In truth, School Choice would save money because it would relieve the upkeep of school buildings and employment of a bloated bureaucracy of teachers unions and school district functionaries. We could allow public schools to exist and receive the tuition or vouchers if parents preferred them. This would require public schools to compete with private schools and homeschooling curricula. The children and families would benefit as institutions improved themselves through healthy competition.

CONCLUSION

Education is one of the most important decisions a Christian family can make. Whether choosing a private Christian school, participating in the School Choice Movement, or homeschooling, the goal is the same: to raise children who love the Lord, pursue truth, and serve others with excellence. In a world that often promotes values contrary to Scripture, Christian education provides a refuge and a foundation for the next generation of believers.

Christian parents, educators, and policymakers must work together to support and expand educational options that honor God and equip students for both earthly success and eternal significance. As Proverbs 1:7 reminds us, "The fear of the Lord is the beginning of knowledge." With this foundation, Christian education can continue to flourish and shape the future for the glory of God.

ACTION ITEMS

1. Build Christian private schools and make them affordable by scaling.
2. Promote School Choice through coupons or waivers that would subsidize Christian schools.
3. Promote homeschooling through coupons or grants that would enable parents to educate their children.
4. Allow for charter schools with Christian affiliations.

STRATEGY 7

PARENTAL RIGHTS OVER CHILDREN

Parental rights stand at the heart of God's design for the family, a sacred institution where mothers and fathers are entrusted as primary stewards of their children's physical, moral, and spiritual well-being. From a Christian Patriot perspective, this authority is not merely a societal construct but a divine mandate, rooted in Scripture and affirmed by Church tradition. Today, however, this God-given role faces unprecedented challenges as governments, schools, and medical establishments assert control over decisions involving vaccines, abortion, transgender transitioning, and religious education. High-profile controversies—like California's 2022 AB 2098, which threatened doctors who opposed vaccine mandates, or the 2023 push for minors' access to gender-affirming care without parental consent—underscore the urgency of defending parental rights. This chapter argues that parents, not the state, hold the primary responsibility to guide their children in these matters, drawing on biblical principles, Catholic doctrine, and modern examples to affirm their authority as guardians of both body and soul.

The New Secular Religion seeks to isolate parents from their children, not only in education but especially in the realm of healthcare. They promote the godless presumption that that the secular state—not the parent—wields the higher authority over a child. For instance, in 2024, Montana's Supreme Court struck down a law requiring parental consent for minors seeking an abortion, affirming the right of minors to make reproductive decisions without parental consent. New Jersey, New Mexico, New York, and Oregon also have similar rules for minors to seek abortion without parental consent or notification.

The same presupposition applies to gender reassignment and mandatory gender-affirming care. Parents who object can be penalized by law. In May 2023, Washington Governor Jay Inslee signed a law designating the state as a "sanctuary" for transgender youth, ensuring that minors can access gender-affirming care without parental consent. One month later, in June 2023, New York Governor Kathy Hochul signed a law protecting access to transition-related medical care for transgender minors, allowing them to receive such care without parental consent. In July 2023, Oregon Governor Tina Kotek signed a law protecting access to abortion and gender-affirming care for transgender youth.

Once again, new secular regulations have replaced those based on Natural Law and Sacred Scripture. The void created by the retreat of Christians has been filled by absolute statism over the minds and hearts of our sons and daughters. To counter this encroachment, Christians must demand medical choice over our families. The concept of medical choice refers to the rights of parents to make informed decisions regarding their children's healthcare, including controversial issues such as gender surgeries, vaccines, and other medical interventions. Christians must advocate for national policies and protections that respect parental medical choices based on the revered status of the family, moral responsibility, the sanctity of life, and the authority of parents in nurturing their children.

PARENTAL RIGHTS OVER CHILDREN'S MEDICAL AND MORAL CARE

Ephesians 6:4 instructs, "And you, fathers, provoke not your children to anger, but bring them up in the discipline and correction of the Lord." This divine call empowers parents to make decisions aligned with God's law, even against secular pressures. As we explore vaccines, abortion, transgender issues, and religious education, we see a consistent truth: parental rights are not optional but essential to fulfilling God's plan.

VACCINES AND PARENTAL CONSCIENCE

Vaccines have sparked fierce debate, especially since the COVID-19 pandemic, with mandates clashing against parental authority. In 2021, Tennessee parents protested when school boards enforced COVID-19 vaccine requirements for students, igniting a legal battle over consent. Similarly, California's 2022 AB 2098 sought to penalize doctors for "misinformation," opposing vaccine orthodoxy and chilling discussions that parents rely on to make informed choices. From a Christian Patriot lens, parents must retain authority here, guided by conscience and faith.

Scripture affirms parental stewardship. Proverbs 22:6 commands, "Train up a child in the way he should go: and when he is old, he will not depart from it." This includes health decisions, where vaccines—while often beneficial—carry risks like rare adverse effects (e.g., myocarditis in teens post-Pfizer, per CDC data).

The 2023 case of Emily Tuttle, a Michigan mother, exemplifies this tension. She refused the MMR vaccine for her son due to religious objections to fetal cell lines, facing school exclusion despite state exemptions. Courts upheld her rights under the First Amendment, reflecting God's delegation of authority to parents, not bureaucrats. Deuteronomy 6:6–7 reinforces this: "And these words which I command thee this day…thou shalt teach them diligently to thy children." When states impose medical choices, they fracture this sacred duty, risking both bodily harm and spiritual erosion.

PARENTAL AUTHORITY AND ABORTION

Abortion pits parental rights against a culture of death, especially when minors seek it without consent. In 2023, Idaho's Defense of Life Act banned abortion outright, but Planned Parenthood challenged it, arguing minors' "autonomy" via judicial bypass—a process upheld in *Bellotti v. Baird* (1979). Christian teaching rejects this, affirming parents as protectors of life.

The 2022 case of a ten-year-old Ohio girl, raped and taken across state lines for an abortion post-Dobbs, horrified many. Her parents, sidelined by activists, lost their chance to guide her through trauma and protect her unborn child. State laws allowing minors' abortions without notification—like California's—violate "Thou shalt not kill," and usurp parental duty. Colossians 3:20–21 balances this: "Children, obey your parents in all things…. Fathers, provoke not your children to indignation," urging mutual respect while affirming authority. Parents must intervene to uphold God's law, not cede it to courts or clinics.

TRANSGENDER AND TRANSITIONING WITH PARENTAL NOTIFICATION

Transgender transitioning for minors—which includes hormone blockers and surgeries—has surged, often without parental consent. In 2023, Washington State's SB 5599 allowed shelters to house teens seeking "gender-affirming care" without notifying parents, sparking outrage. Christians see this as a rejection of God's created order, with parents as stewards of their children's identity.

Genesis 1:27 states, "Male and female he created them," a binary affirmed by Christ in Matthew 19:4: "Have ye not read, that he who made man from the beginning, made them male and female?" The *Catechism of the Catholic Church* (2333) teaches that "everyone, man and woman, should acknowledge and accept his sexual identity." Puberty blockers, linked to sterility risks (per a 2022 NIH study) and mastectomies for teens defy this, altering bodies God designed. Parents must guide children through confusion, not surrender them to ideology.

The 2021 case of Keira Bell in the UK, who regretted her transition after blockers at age sixteen, highlights the stakes. Her parents, uninformed by clinics, couldn't protect her—a tragedy echoing in US battles like Virginia's 2023 Sage's Law, where a teen runaway received hormones against parental wishes. Ephesians 6:1–4 calls parents to "bring them up in the discipline and correction of the Lord," a duty undermined when states prioritize "autonomy" over truth. Catholic bioethics, per the *Ethical and Religious Directives for Catholic Health Care Services* (US Conference of Catholic Bishops, 2018), rejects such interventions as mutilation, entrusting parents to safeguard their child's God-given nature.

LGBTQ+ EDUCATION

Religious education faces encroachment as schools push secular curricula over parental values. In 2023, Maryland's Montgomery County Schools banned opt-outs from LGBTQ+ lessons, clashing with Christian parents' beliefs. The 2021 Loudoun County, Virginia, protests saw parents decry Critical Race Theory and sexual content overriding their faith-based teachings. Courts have wavered—*Pierce v. Society of Sisters* (1925) upheld private religious schooling—yet modern policies erode such freedoms. Matthew 18:6 warns, "But he that shall scandalize one of these little ones...it were better for him that a millstone should be hanged about his neck." Parents must shield children from teachings contradicting Christ, a right states increasingly challenge. Pressure can be placed on teachers, school boards, and local leaders, but often parents must opt out and seek Christian schools or homeschool as the only safe solution.

CONCLUSION

Parental rights over vaccines, abortion, transgender transitioning, and religious education are not mere preferences but a sacred trust from God. Modern controversies—vaccine mandates, minors' abortions, gender interventions, and secular indoctrination—reveal a state overreach that Christian Patriots reject. Scripture and tradition unite in this defense. 1 Timothy 5:8 declares, "But if any man have not care of his own...he hath denied the faith," tying stewardship to salvation. Whether resisting California's vaccine laws, protecting a daughter from abortion, guiding a son through gender confusion, or teaching Christ's truth, parents fulfill a divine vocation. Modern battles demand vigilance—joining groups like the Parental Rights Foundation or voting for faith-aligned leaders—but the foundation remains eternal: "As for me and my house, we will serve the Lord" (Joshua 24:15). This is not about control but love—love for God's law, for children's bodies, and for their eternal souls. Christian Patriots must stand firm, trusting that Christ, who said, "Suffer the little children to come unto me" (Mark 10:14), honors parents who guard His little ones.

ACTION ITEMS

1. Identify state overreach violating parental notification for abortion, sex education, transgender transition, and LGBTQ+ indoctrination.
2. Fight locally and in the courts.
3. Seek representatives who will overturn, fight, and defund platforms that work around parental consent in public institutions.

STRATEGY 8

PORNOGRAPHY MADE ILLEGAL

"It's like an addiction. You keep craving something that is harder, harder, something which gives you a greater sense of excitation—until you reach a point where the pornography only goes so far, and then you start looking for other ways to satisfy that."[1]

—Serial killer Ted Bundy on the effect of pornography on his life

Pornography, once confined to shadowy corners, now floods the digital world, infiltrating homes and hearts with a click. The Christian Patriot understands that it is not mere entertainment but a corrosive force that ravages souls, fractures families, and undermines God's design for human dignity. *The Catechism of the Catholic Church* defines pornography as a sin that "offends against chastity" and "does grave injury to the dignity of its participants" (2354), a stance rooted in Christ's call to purity in Matthew 5:8: "Blessed are the clean of heart: for they shall see God."

Today, over 4 billion pornographic web pages thrive online, per 2023 Internet filtering data, ensnaring millions—many as young as eleven, according to Common Sense Media. The Christian Patriot laments pornography's spiritual desolation and psychological devastation. He demands its legal prohibition online by all nations. Some countries, like Pakistan and Saudi Arabia, have already acted, but the global response remains tepid. Scripture, tradition, and evidence compel Christians to advocate for a world where this plague is eradicated from the digital sphere.

Pornography's ubiquity on smartphones, tablets, and laptops amplifies its harm, making it a public health crisis cloaked as personal freedom. Proverbs 6:25 warns, "Be not taken with her beauty, and be not caught with her winking eyes," a timeless caution against lust's lure. The Church, echoing St. Paul in 1 Corinthians 6:19—"Know you not, that your members are the temple of the Holy Ghost?"—sees the body as sacred, not a commodity. This chapter explores why pornography destroys lives and why nations must unite to ban it online, following the lead of those already taking steps.

A WAR ON THE SOUL

Pornography wages war on the soul, severing humanity's bond with God. Jesus teaches in Matthew 5:28, "Whosoever shall look on a woman to lust after her, hath already committed adultery with her in his heart." This sin of the heart, magnified by pornography's endless stream, drags souls from grace. Saint Augustine, in *Confessions*, laments his own bondage to lust: "The enemy held my will...and thence had made a chain for me" (Book VIII). Today's data mirrors this enslavement—Pornhub's 2023 report logged 130 million daily visitors, many habitual users.[2] A 2022 study from the *Journal of Behavioral Addictions* found that 17 percent of users exhibit compulsive pornography consumption, which correlates with spiritual emptiness—church attendance drops, guilt festers, and faith withers.

For Christians, the body is a temple, not a tool for exploitation. 1 Thessalonians 4:3–4 urges, "This is the will of God, your sanctification: that you should abstain from fornication; that every one of you should know how to possess his vessel in sanctification and honour." Pornography profanes this, commodifying God's image-bearers (Genesis 1:27). Early Church Fathers like Tertullian, in *On Modesty*, condemned lewd spectacles, a precursor to today's digital vice. Its spiritual toll—alienation from God, fractured prayer, and hardened hearts—demands its ban, lest souls perish in silence.

PSYCHOLOGICAL DEVASTATION

Pornography's psychological wreckage is profound, rewiring minds and shattering well-being. Neuroscience confirms this: a 2021 Cambridge University study showed excessive pornography use alters brain reward systems, akin to drug addiction, reducing gray matter in areas tied to impulse control. Users chase escalating content, with 88 percent of top porn scenes depicting aggression, per a 2020 Violence Against Women analysis. This distorts reality, as St. Paul warns in Romans 12:2, "Be not conformed to this world; but be reformed in the newness of your mind."

The fallout is stark. A 2023 American Psychological Association report linked pornography to anxiety, depression, and sexual dysfunction in 30 percent of frequent users. Men, 70 percent of whom view it monthly per Barna Group data, report shame and isolation—echoing Psalm 37:4, "My iniquities are grown above my head: and as a heavy burden they are become heavy upon me." Women, too, suffer; 34 percent feel pressured to mimic pornographic acts per a 2022 *Journal of Sex Research* study, eroding self-worth. Teens, exposed at an average age of eleven (NSPCC, 2023), face warped expectations—40 percent show risky sexual behavior, per *Pediatrics*.

High-profile cases of pornography amplify its danger as it crosses into total dehumanization of its victims. Ted Bundy, the serial killer, claimed in a 1989 interview that pornography fueled his violent fantasies, a chilling testament to its power to dehumanize.

> "Like most other kinds of addiction, I would keep looking for more potent, more explicit, more graphic kinds of material. Like an addiction, you keep craving something which is harder, harder, something which gives you a greater sense of excitement—until you reach the point where the pornography only goes so far, that jumping-off point where you begin to wonder if maybe actually doing it will give you that which is beyond just reading about it or looking at it.... I've lived in prison a long time now. I've met a lot of men who were motivated to commit violence just like me. And without exception, every one of them was deeply involved in pornography."[3]

Jeffrey Dahmer, the cannibalistic homosexual killer of seventeen men and boys between 1978 and 1991 also spoke of the role of pornography in his degenerate murders:

> "Just...using pictures of past victims, the pornography videos, the magazines.... It just gets in your mind and stays there. It's a gradual thing—it doesn't happen overnight. But once it's in there, it's hard to get rid of it, and it fueled what I did."[4]

Serial killer Edmund Kemper, murderer of ten victims, including his mother, spoke to the role of pornography in his own crimes:

> "I had these detective magazines and pornography that I'd look at...it was erotic stimulation at first, but then it turned into something else. I'd fantasize about the women in them, and then about what I'd do to them—killing them, cutting them up. It started there, and it grew."[5]

Arthur Shawcross, who killed fourteen people between 1972 and 1989, spoke about pornography's maddening influence on him during a 1990 interview with criminologist Dr. Joel Norris. He linked his exposure to pornographic magazines with his violent sexual impulses.

> "I'd look at those pictures—dirty magazines, you know—and it'd get me going. It wasn't just looking; it was thinking about what I could do to them, the girls in the pictures. It made me want to hurt somebody, and I did."[6]

These depraved minds began by *sexually objectifying* other people through pornography. Their minds were warped sexually through pornographic materials so the people depicted in pornography are no longer *really* people. This dehumanization of the other through pornography naturally led to their dehumanization in the act of murder. Sexual perversion and rape is forcing your will on another. Murder is just the next step.

FAMILIAL AND SOCIETAL DECAY

Pornography slashes society's fabric, starting with the family—God's cornerstone. Genesis 2:24 states, "Wherefore a man shall leave father and mother, and shall cleave to his wife: and they shall be two in one flesh." Pornography betrays this union. A 2023 *Journal of Family Issues* study found 56 percent of divorces cite pornography as a factor, with infidelity and mistrust surging among users.[7] Ephesians 5:25 commands, "Husbands, love your wives, as Christ also loved the church," yet pornography fosters selfishness, not sacrifice.

Children suffer most. The US Department of Justice (2022) links pornography exposure to a 300 percent rise in teen sexual violence.[8] Schools report "sexting" scandals—like the 2023 Virginia case where one hundred students faced charges—tracing back to pornographic norms. Proverbs 22:6 implores, "Train up a child in the way he should go," but online access subverts this, with 70 percent of kids encountering porn unintentionally (Internet Matters, 2023). Communities crumble as empathy erodes; a 2021 *Social Science Quarterly* study tied pornography to increased acceptance of exploitation.

Some nations recognize pornography's harm, enacting online bans, though enforcement varies. Pakistan, since 2011, has blocked over 400,000 pornographic sites via the Pakistan Telecommunication Authority, citing Islamic values and public morality—punishments include fines up to 1 million rupees. Saudi Arabia's "Great Firewall" filters all pornography, aligning with Sharia law; violators face lashings or jail. China's Golden Shield Project, active since 2002, censors porn alongside dissent, with fines up to $2,200 for VPN use. Thailand's 2019 ban targets online adult content, imposing up to five years' imprisonment. North Korea, with total internet control, bans pornography outright, though internet access is near-impossible regardless.

These efforts, while imperfect—VPNs often bypass blocks—signal a precedent. Western nations lag, prioritizing "free speech" over moral clarity. The UK's 2019 Age Verification Act stalled, leaving children exposed. The US, despite First Amendment protections, saw Utah declare pornography a "public health crisis" in 2016, a symbolic step. Scripture demands more. Matthew 18:6 thunders, "He that shall scandalize one of these little ones...it were better for him that a millstone should be hanged about his neck." Nations must act, as Romans 13:4 affirms rulers as "God's ministers" for justice.

A global online ban is feasible—internet governance bodies like ICANN could blacklist domains, ISPs could filter content, and treaties could unify enforcement. The Catholic Church, in the Pontifical Council for Social Communications (2000), urged laws against "pornographic exploitation." Christians must lobby, leveraging examples like Pakistan's resolve, to protect the vulnerable.

CONCLUSION

Pornography is no benign pastime but a destroyer of lives—spiritually, psychologically, and socially. It desolates souls, chaining them to lust rather than God's grace (1 Corinthians 6:18: "Avoid fornication"). It devastates minds, breeding addiction and despair (Romans 12:2). It unravels families and communities, defying God's plan (Genesis 2:24). Nations like Pakistan, Saudi Arabia, and China model restriction: Why can't Christian states and nations do the same? The Bible's call is clear—2 Timothy 2:22 urges, "Fly from the desires of youth, and follow justice, faith, charity, and peace." Pornography's online flood demands a dam before the next generation is drowned in degeneracy.

Christian Patriots bear witness to Christ's mercy and justice. St. Paul's plea in Philippians 4:8—"Whatsoever things are true, whatsoever modest...think on these things"—is a blueprint for culture. The recent rise in "quit porn" and "no fap" movements, like Reclaim Recovery, shows hearts yearning for freedom. Yet individual resolve needs legal teeth. A global ban, rooted in love for God's image-bearers, is not censorship but salvation—a shield for the weak, a call to holiness. As Psalm 118:37 prays, "Turn away my eyes that they may not behold vanity," so must nations turn from this plague, restoring dignity to all.

ACTION ITEMS

1. Preach and teach that pornography is sinful.
2. Install software and protections at home to prevent pornography.
3. Copy the initiatives of Pakistan, Saudi Arabia, China, and North Korea in their ability to block pornographic sites.

STRATEGY 9

END HUMAN TRAFFICKING AND CHILD EXPLOITATION

We often think of slavery as something of the past—a human injustice solved by previous generations. Most people are unaware that there are now more enslaved people on Earth than ever before. According to the International Labour Organization (ILO), there are now approximately 27.6 million people in forced labor globally. Of this total, 6.3 million were victims of forced sexual exploitation, which includes sex slavery such as prostitution and pornography production coerced through force, fraud, or violence. This figure encompasses both adults and children, with women and girls making up the vast majority—99 percent of victims in the commercial sex industry, per the ILO.[1] Slavery is not a forgotten and abolished practice—it is one of the greatest injustices of our time.

In the heart of every Christian lies the echo of Christ's teaching: "Whatever you did for one of the least of these brothers and sisters of mine, you did for me" (Matthew 25:40). Yet across the globe and even within our own communities, millions of God's children are ensnared by the invisible chains of human trafficking and exploitation. This modern-day slavery—often cloaked in the shadows of prostitution, pornography, and forced labor—strips people of their God-given dignity and mocks the sanctity of life. As

Christian Patriots, we are called not only to mourn this injustice but to act against it with compassion and courage.

The problem is only getting worse. Of the 27.6 million enslaved, 6.3 million were forced into commercial sexual exploitation as of 2022. Earlier ILO estimates from 2016 found the number at 4.8 million, indicating a significant rise over six years from 2016 to 2022. Global crises like the COVID-19 pandemic, armed conflicts, and economic instability are factors for this increase. The primary variable, however, is the increase in human immigration. The fragility of national borders and the careless transition of children and young adults through dangerous regions and cloudy national policies makes them especially vulnerable.

IMMIGRATION AND 323,000 MISSING YOUTH

According to a 2024 report from the Department of Homeland Security (DHS), US Immigration and Customs Enforcement (ICE) could not account for the locations of approximately 32,000 unaccompanied migrant children after they were released from federal custody under the Biden presidency.[2] The report notes that these children were processed at the US–Mexico border, primarily as unaccompanied minors, and then lost contact with federal oversight, raising concerns about potential exploitation or trafficking. Sadly, the numbers are far greater.

Tom Homan, former Acting Director of ICE and incoming border czar under the Trump administration, has gone on record testifying that approximately 323,000 migrant children have gone missing from 2019 to 2023. This number aligns with a February 2024 letter from Republican lawmakers citing HHS data, which indicated that ORR lost contact with around 85,000 children out of 291,000 placed with sponsors from 2021 to 2023, with estimates suggesting the total could exceed 300,000 when accounting for earlier years and unreported cases.

Globally, children are a substantial portion of those trafficked illegally, with over 1.2 million minors estimated to be victims of sexual exploitation at any time, according to Save the Children's 2024 data.[3] This number confirms ILO's findings that 27 percent of all trafficking victims are children. These numbers are conservative because trafficking often goes unreported, and data collection is limited in conflict zones, authoritarian regimes, and regions with weak law enforcement. The United Nations Office on Drugs and Crime notes that sexual exploitation remains the most detected form of trafficking globally, accounting for 50 percent of identified cases in their 2024 Global Report on Trafficking in Persons, down from 54 percent in 2016, suggesting some shift toward other forms like forced labor but still revealing a global crisis.[4]

SEXUAL EXPLOITATION: $173 BILLION PER YEAR

Abuse doesn't just occur through human trafficking. The Polaris Project, which operates the National Human Trafficking Hotline, received reports of 10,359 trafficking situations in 2022, affecting an estimated 16,554 victims. Of these, 60 percent of identified child sex trafficking victims in the US had a history in the child welfare system, underscoring the vulnerability of foster children. The National Center for Missing and Exploited Children reported 88 million files of child sexual abuse material in 2022 alone, a chilling indicator of the scale of child exploitation. The US Department of State's 2024 Trafficking in Persons Report notes that the federal government prosecuted 1,026 human trafficking cases in 2023, resulting in 1,025 convictions—yet these numbers represent only a fraction of the true crisis.[5]

The commercial sex industry, including prostitution and pornography, drives much of this trafficking. Forced sexual exploitation generates $173 billion in illegal profits annually worldwide, making it the second most profitable illegal industry in the US, surpassed only by drug trafficking. The internet has amplified the problem, with an estimated 500,000 predators active online daily, using social media platforms to recruit and exploit minors, according to advocacy groups like Our Rescue. Pornography, often viewed as a separate issue, is deeply intertwined: a 2020 investigation revealed that major pornography websites hosted content derived from trafficking victims, including children, prompting companies like Visa and Mastercard to sever ties with sites like Pornhub after it deleted 10 million videos overnight.

It is easy to get lost in the data points. We must ponder in our hearts that these numbers are people. Each and every one of them is created in God's image, with hopes and dreams. Each statistic represents a child lured by a pervert feigning trust, a woman coerced into selling her body for the profit of a pimp, or a man trapped in labor bondage. Their innocence and dignity is ripped away. We cannot stand by idly. For the Christian Patriot, this is a call to action rooted in the biblical mandate to "rescue those being led away to death" (Proverbs 24:11).

THE BIBLE AND HUMAN OPPRESSION

Scripture is unequivocal about God's stance on exploitation. The prophet Isaiah declares, "Learn to do right; seek justice. Defend the oppressed. Take up the cause of the fatherless; plead the case of the widow" (Isaiah 1:17). The Psalms proclaim God as a "father to the fatherless, a defender of widows" (Psalm 67:6), and Jesus Himself began His ministry by quoting Isaiah: "The Spirit of the Lord is on me, because he has anointed me to proclaim good news to the poor...to set the oppressed free" (Luke 4:18). Human trafficking is an affront to God's design for humanity, a perversion of relationships meant to reflect love, honor, and mutual care.

The Bible also confronts the sins that fuel trafficking. Pornography and prostitution thrive on degenerate lust, which Jesus equates with adultery in the heart (Matthew 5:28). The exploitation of children echoes the warning of Christ: "If anyone causes one of these little ones who believe in me to stumble, it would be better for them to have a millstone hung around their neck and to be drowned in the depths of the sea" (Matthew 18:6). Christ calls for death; not rehabilitation. For the Christian Patriot, trafficking is not just a sin; it is a crime against God, society, and, most of all, the enslaved.

THE CONNECTION BETWEEN PROSTITUTION, PORNOGRAPHY, AND TRAFFICKING

To address human trafficking, Christian Patriots must recognize its deep ties to prostitution and pornography. The United Nations Palermo Protocol defines trafficking as the recruitment or harboring of persons through force, fraud, or coercion for exploitation, including prostitution and sexual exploitation. Yet, as *Christian Concern* notes, the line between "voluntary" prostitution and trafficking is often illusory—most women and children in prostitution face violence, coercion, drug abuse, and psychological trauma, regardless of how they entered "the trade." Studies show that 70–75 percent of prostitutes are survivors of childhood sexual abuse, and in the US, the average age of entry into the sex trade is twelve to fourteen, according to The Heritage Foundation.[6,7]

Pornography exacerbates this cycle. Catherine MacKinnon, a legal scholar, observes that "pornography is one way women and children are trafficked for sex."[8] The normalization of pornography in culture desensitizes society to exploitation, creating demand that traffickers meet through supply—often children. In 2023, the FBI recovered child trafficking victims, 60 percent of whom were from foster care or group homes, many exploited in pornography or prostitution rings.

PREVENTION AND EDUCATION

Most of the data available on human trafficking is based on numbers pertaining to the United States of America, as Christians have become more aware of the problem within and on our borders. American Christians, numbering over 200 million, wield significant influence through their faith, resources, and collective voice. Here are four practical, biblically grounded ways to combat human trafficking and child exploitation:

1. **Close and Control Borders.** The largest amount of missing persons and human trafficking are found on the borders and in border towns. Illegal and undocumented immigration may seem "compassionate," but it fosters illegal activity in the form of drug running and human enslavement. Vulnerable people are at the mercy of cartels and mafias who trade not only in narcotics but also in prostitution. Millions of young people (and adults) are coerced into prostitution and pornography by force and false promises. A secure border removes the shadows under which human trafficking thrives.
2. **Intercessory Prayer.** Christians are called to be "salt and light" (Matthew 5:13–16), preserving righteousness and

illuminating darkness. Advocacy is a powerful tool to dismantle the systems that enable trafficking. In the US, policies like the Trafficking Victims Protection Act (TVPA) of 2000 have made strides, yet gaps remain. For instance, the 2024 Trafficking in Persons Report highlights that victims are still arrested for acts committed under coercion, and labor trafficking remains under-addressed. Christians can lobby for stronger laws—such as criminalizing the purchase of sex, as in Sweden's model, which reduced trafficking inflows—or mandating trafficking screenings in foster care and immigration systems.

3. **Compassion and Aid to the Victims.** Jesus modeled compassion for the broken, dining with tax collectors and prostitutes (Luke 15:1–2). Christians can follow His example by supporting trafficking survivors with tangible aid. The 2024 Trafficking in Persons Report notes a dire shortage of housing and specialized services for survivors in the US, with funding for victim services lagging behind need. Churches can fill this gap by creating safe houses, offering job training, or funding counseling rooted in Christian love. Faith-based groups like A21 and International Justice Mission (IJM) rescue victims and provide aftercare, often with church support. In 2022, IJM helped liberate 1,500 people globally, many through partnerships with local congregations. American Christians can donate, volunteer, or adopt a "rescue and restore" ministry, ensuring survivors know they are valued as "fearfully and wonderfully made" (Psalm 139:14). Addressing root causes—like the 60 percent of child victims from foster care—means mentoring at-risk youth or becoming foster parents to prevent exploitation.

4. **Education and Prevention.** The demand for prostitution and pornography fuels trafficking, and Christians must confront this sin within their own ranks. A 2019 Barna study found that 54 percent of practicing Christian men and 15 percent of Christian women admitted to viewing pornography monthly. This is deeply-rooted hypocrisy. Those that consume pornography are directly supporting evil and incentivizing human trafficking, whether they know it or not. The Apostle Paul urges believers to "flee from sexual immorality" (1 Corinthians 6:18), and pastors should regularly preach against the grave sins of prostitution and pornography. Woe to the man or woman who stands before God on judgment day as an enabler in one of the world's greatest evils. Christian parents, pastors, and youth leaders must also educate their children about the 500,000 perverted predators lurking online daily. Parents must lock down their internet and devices and tell their children never to chat or correspond with strangers online.

CONCLUSION

Human trafficking and child exploitation are not insurmountable. With 27.6 million victims worldwide, 88 million CSAM files reported, and $173 billion in illicit profits, the numbers are daunting—but the God we serve is greater. Christians in America, armed with faith, prayer, and action, can lead the charge to end this evil. By advocating for justice, supporting survivors, and confronting cultural sin, we embody Christ's love and fulfill Micah 6:8: "To act justly and to love mercy and to walk humbly with your God." The road is long, but our resolve must be unshakable, for in rescuing the least of these, we serve the One who came to set the captives free.

ACTION ITEMS

1. Advocate for closed and controlled borders.
2. Pray for an end to human trafficking and pray for the victims.
3. Provide counseling, spiritual rehabilitation, and housing for those rescued from the industry.
4. Educate and preach against prostitution and pornography.
5. Warn our children of the dangers of predators and install software to protect them.

STRATEGY 10

JUST WAR AND FOREIGN POLICY

Christians have not been, and are not, pacifists. Some often cite Christ's teaching to "turn the other cheek," found in Matthew 5:38–39 as proof that Christians are nonviolent and opposed to armed conflict. Our Lord delivered this command in his Sermon on the Mount within the full context of "You have heard that it was said, 'Eye for eye, and tooth for tooth.' But I tell you, do not resist an evil person. If anyone slaps you on the right cheek, turn to them the other cheek also." Christ challenges the false presumption of *personal* retributive justice (Exodus 21:24). Christ and the Father are one, and the Bible shows that physical violence and war are not merely tolerated but mandated by God. Throughout Christian history, Christians have justified wars and violence—often labeled "just"—in ways they argue align with broader biblical principles.

CONTEXT AND MEANING OF "TURN THE OTHER CHEEK"

To understand Jesus' words, we must consider their historical and cultural backdrop. In 1st-century Judea, under Roman occupation, a slap on the right cheek—likely delivered with the back of the right hand—was a profound insult, symbolizing humiliation rather than lethal aggression. By instructing followers to offer the other cheek, Jesus wasn't addressing life-threatening violence, but rather personal disrespect. Alongside commands to "love your enemies" (Matthew 5:44) and "do not resist an evil person," this suggests a radical ethic of nonviolent resistance, rooted in trust in God's justice over human vengeance.

For early Christians, this teaching shaped a largely pacifist stance in their personal lives. Christians did not enjoy civil protections and did not hold public office or authority. The pre-Constantinian church (before AD 313) was marked by Christians emulating Christ's nonresistance, even unto martyrdom. After Constantine, Christianity was not only tolerated, but it became the state religion of the Roman Empire, Armenia, and more nations throughout the centuries. This raised the question of the propriety of righteous violence and just war theory.

BIBLICAL FOUNDATION FOR JUST VIOLENCE

While Jesus' personal example—allowing his arrest and crucifixion without resistance—reinforces "turn the other cheek," other biblical passages reveal a justification for just wars and violence. The Old Testament depicts God commanding violence, such as the conquest of Canaan (Joshua 6–12) and the punishment of evildoers (Psalm 149:6–9). Christians arguing for just war often see these as divine endorsements of force to uphold righteousness, suggesting Jesus' teaching on the mount applies to personal ethics, not state or communal defense.

In the New Testament, the Apostle Paul taught: "For he [the emperor or governor] is God's minister to thee, for good. But if thou do that which is evil, fear: for he beareth not the sword in vain. For he is God's minister: an avenger to execute wrath upon him that doth evil" (Romans 13:4). If the Apostle perceived pagan kings as "God's minister...an avenger" how much more so the Christian king? According to the New Testament, God ordains governments to wield force against evil, distinguishing personal nonviolence from collective justice. Early Christian thinkers like Augustine leaned on this to argue that Christians could serve in such roles without violating Jesus' command to "turn the other cheek."

VIOLENCE TO PROTECT THE INNOCENT

Christ's teaching that "Greater love has no one than this: to lay down one's life for one's friends" (John 15:13) extends to justify defending the weak. If an enemy torments or even kills me for hatred of my faith and Christ, I bear it in accordance with His grace and fulfill the teaching of Christ. However, if an enemy attacks my children, my wife, the elderly, or the vulnerable, I have a duty to protect them and use force—even violent force. One might ask whether we can use violent force to protect ourselves. The Christian tradition answers affirmatively with a caveat. If one is being attacked on account of hatred of Christ and our faith in Christ, we are called to die as martyrs. However, if the attack is not prompted by hatred of Christ and our faith, for example, in a bank robbery or home intrusion, we may use deadly force to protect our life and the lives of those around us.

Saint Thomas Aquinas explains the distinction that "it is lawful for a man to defend his own life" and that "one is not bound to abstain from all violence in order to preserve one's life."[1] He bases this on Natural Law—the inherent right to preserve one's existence, which he sees as God-given. Aquinas introduces the concept of "double effect" to justify killing in self-defense, stating that the primary effect is to protect oneself. The lower, secondary effect is to harm or kill the attacker. If someone uses force chiefly to protect himself and, as a result, kills the attacker, it's permissible, provided the primary intent is self-preservation, not murder. This principle of double effect extends from personal security to communal and national security.

AUGUSTINE AND THE JUST WAR TRADITION

The Christian theologian who provided the most advanced and systematic theology of righteous violence and just war was Saint Augustine of Hippo (AD 354–430). As a bishop living in the Christian Roman Empire, Augustine grappled with barbarian invasions and internal disorder, that dismantled civil stability. In his monumental work *The City of God*, Augustine argued that violence and war could be justified if they met three criteria:[2]

1. **Violence with right intent (e.g., love, not vengeance).** War must be waged with the chief effect of protecting one's people or a persecuted people. Revenge or malice are not conditions for just war.
2. **Exercised by right authority.** A private citizen cannot become a vigilante and hunt down the wicked. Acts of violence must ordinarily be accomplished by those legally deputized to enforce violence. For example, a Texas border town cannot rightfully declare war on a Mexican border town.
3. **Having a just cause.** The declaration of war must be provoked by a just cause. Violent war cannot be sparked by land grabs, the desire for cheap oil, or factors that would economically favor corporations. There must be an actual threat to the nation and its citizens.

Over time, two more conditions were added:

1. **As a last resort.** Thomas Aquinas added that war is lawful only when "there is no other way" to secure peace, though he didn't phrase it as explicitly as modern doctrine. Negotiations should always precede violence or war *if possible.*[3]
2. **Probability of Success.** Aquinas added that there must be a reasonable hope that violence or war will end with the intended outcome of success unto peace.[4] In other words, a nation with an army of 25,000 and no tanks should not declare and initiate war against an antagonist with 500,000 troops and advanced machinery. It's a fool's war with blood spilled for no positive outcome. Saint Augustine also stipulated this condition elsewhere, where he noted that war should aim for "peace as the end," implying a balance of outcomes.[5]

Christian Patriots must understand and digest our traditional just war theory and *insist* that national conflicts meet the conditions of just war. As a father of military-aged sons, my wife and I do not want our children to die on foreign beaches or in jungles for conflicts designed to line the pockets of corporations. The United States of America should rethink her international alliances and study the causes and outcomes of political unrest globally. The slogan that "we must support our allies at all costs," is not in line with just war theory. Sending soldiers to die over rumors of "weapons of mass destruction" does not fall under just war theory. Supporting NATO for the sake of NATO does not meet the conditions of just war theory. One key condition to just war theory is that legitimate authority must invoke war—are foreign nations in a place to initiate war on our behalf? No. Instead, the Christian Patriot must infuse political discourse and military policy with the righteous and noble tradition that Christians have sought to follow (sometimes unsuccessfully) to only engage in war when it meets the conditions of just war.

ACTION ITEMS

1. Pastors and leaders should educate their flocks about the Christian tradition of just war theory.
2. Elect Christian leaders who promise to defend our nation in accordance with this proper theological framework.
3. Ratify that all wars must be ratified by Congress. End all stealth wars and "unofficial wars" without end.

STRATEGY 11

FOREIGN AID FOR PERSECUTED CHRISTIANS

Related to just war theory is the concept of foreign aid and international assistance. Christ's parable of the Good Samaritan compels us to aid those in distress, regardless of borders or ethnicity, as a matter of loving our neighbor:

> But he, wanting to justify himself, said to Jesus, 'And who is my neighbor?'
>
> And Jesus answering, said: A certain man went down from Jerusalem to Jericho, and fell among robbers, who also stripped him, and having wounded him, went away, leaving him half dead. And it chanced that a certain priest went down the same way, and seeing him, passed by. In like manner, also a Levite, when he was near the place and saw him, passed by. But a certain Samaritan, being on his journey, came near him; and seeing him, was moved with compassion. And going up to him, bound up his wounds, pouring in oil and wine, and setting him upon his own beast, brought him to an inn, and took care of him. And the next day he took out two denarii, and gave to the host, and said: 'Take care of him and whatsoever thou shalt spend over and above, I, at my return, will repay thee.'

> Which of these three, in thy opinion, was neighbor to him that fell among the robbers? And he said: 'He that showed mercy to him.' And Jesus said to him: 'Go, and do thou in like manner.' (Luke 10:29-37)

Christ's parable establishes the Christian Patriot's obligation to alleviate suffering; however, in our political policies regarding immigration, foreign aid, and international distress, the discussion about political *prioritization* becomes inevitable.

In the context of immigration and foreign aid, American Vice President J.D. Vance opened a public debate on the Christian responsibility of "loving locally" by appealing to the traditional *Ordo Amoris* (Latin for "Order of Love") taught by Saint Augustine. On January 29, 2025, Vance told Sean Hannity in a Fox News interview: "There's this old-school, very Christian concept—you love your family, then your neighbor, then your community, then your fellow citizens, and then the rest of the world." Vance, a convert to Catholicism who had chosen Saint Augustine as his confirmation patron, sought to inject ancient Christian nuance into a hot-button debate.

Many Christians lauded Vance; however, others expressed concern that his interpretation of Augustine might restrict Christian love or altogether negate the parable of the Good Samaritan. Notably, Cardinal Robert Prevost, who shortly thereafter became Pope Leo XIV, subtly countersigned J.D. Vance's claim by posting on X an article titled "JD Vance is wrong: Jesus doesn't ask us to rank our love for others" by Kat Armas.[1] Pope Leo XIV, himself an Augustinian friar, subtly cautioned against Vance's ranking of love to the exclusion of loving all. Perhaps the first American Pope and the Catholic Vice President, both of whom are profound admirers of Augustine, will bring nuance to this debate in years to come.

LOVING YOUR NEIGHBOR

Augustine's *City of God* (19.14) defines virtue as loving objects in their proper order—God first, then self, family, and others—while Thomas Aquinas allows flexibility when, for example, urgent need might prioritize a stranger over a relative.[1] Critics have argued Vance rigidified this into a nationalist dogma, ignoring Aquinas' caveat.[2]

In his own words, Augustine explains the ordo amoris as "doing good to everyone he can reach." Here is the pertinent passage from Augustine's *City of God*:

> But as this divine Master [Christ] teaches two commands—the love of God and the love of our neighbor—and as in these commands a man finds three things he has to love: God, himself, and his neighbor. Now he who loves God loves himself thereby, and it follows that he must endeavor to move his neighbor to love God, since he is ordered to love his neighbor as himself. He ought to do the same for his wife, his children, his household, all within his reach, even as he would wish his neighbor to do the same for him if he needed it; and consequently, he will be at peace, or in well-ordered concord, with all men, as far as in him lies.
>
> And this is the order of this concord that a man, in the first place, injure no one, and, in the second, do good to everyone he can reach. Primarily, therefore, his own household is his care, for the law of nature and of society gives him readier access to them and greater opportunity of serving them. And hence the Apostle [Paul] says, "Now, if any provide not for his own, and especially for those of his own house, he has denied the faith, and is worse than an infidel." (*City of God* 19.14)

By carefully summarizing Augustine and adding in the caveat of Aquinas that the Christian may and should sometimes prioritize a stranger over a relative, a proper understanding of ordinary Christian love may be ordered but never made formally exclusive of a class of people. An obligation to love my children cannot exclude my love for all.

A proper Christian *ordo amoris* may look like this. Love for:

1. God
2. my spouse
3. my family, children, and parents
4. my godchildren and extended family
5. my friends and coworkers
6. my neighborhood/community
7. my county
8. my state
9. my nation
10. my nation's allies
11. all nations

Common sense reveals this to be true. I pay for the food, housing, and utilities of my wife and children. Before bed, I pray with them and give them hugs and kisses. I pay local taxes for my county and district. If I work extra hours, I work to benefit my employer, not an unrelated corporation. If I serve in the military, I serve my nation's military, not that of NATO, Russia, Ukraine, or Israel. As Christian Patriots, we hold goodwill and love for all people and all nations. We seek to provide the common good for all. However, with limited time and resources, there is an "order of love" that may be socially defined as an "order of duty." A well-ordered society demands this. Nevertheless, the Christian cannot shirk off love and assistance for those in need or exclude the universal call to love. If a wounded man were to appear on my doorstep, I could not ignore him, with the excuse that I am preparing dinner for my children. We are called to be Good Samaritans and lovingly heal even when it is inconvenient or interrupts our natural obligations.

FOREIGN AID FOR PERSECUTED CHRISTIANS

The debate on *ordo amoris* is related to the newly revealed governmental waste. New scrutiny has revealed that the $58 billion budget of USAID in America is wasted on foreign projects that work against our values. For example:

- $15 million for a Syrian "Sesame Street" remake for Syrian children
- $20 million in "contraceptives" for Taliban-controlled regions
- $50 million for EcoHealth Alliance's bat research redux
- $100 million in "Green Energy" grants to corrupt regimes resulting in half-built projects and no results
- $10 million for Peruvian transgender workshops

This is only a fraction of the waste in our foreign aid. Christians should be prioritizing our foreign aid to assist persecuted Christians. The US, with its Christian majority and global influence, can lead by example, redirecting aid from nations that oppress Christians to those where the Church struggles. This aligns with the principle of stewardship—using resources to glorify God and advance His kingdom. Historically, nations with Christian roots have forged bonds based on shared faith, as seen in the transatlantic ties between Europe and America. Today, aligning with countries that uphold Christian principles, family values, and moral governance—can strengthen a global network to resist secularism and persecution. Such alliances need not exclude others but should prioritize partners who resonate with America's Christian identity, fostering a coalition that defends faith under siege. This approach counters the narrative of isolationism or cultural relativism. While all nations deserve respect, strategic partnerships with those sharing a Christian worldview can amplify efforts to protect religious liberty worldwide. This is not about imposing Christianity but about standing with those who share its ethical foundations, creating a bulwark against ideologies that reject God's truth.

Take, for example, Nigeria. Nigerian Christians face escalating violence from extremist Islamic groups like Boko Haram and Fulani herdsmen. Thousands have been killed and entire villages razed, with estimates suggesting over 10,000 Christian deaths in recent years due to faith-based attacks. Aid here could fund security for Christian communities, support displaced families, and rebuild churches. An alliance with Nigeria's government, if it commits to protecting minorities, could enhance regional stability while uplifting the persecuted Church.

In India, rising Hindu nationalism has led to attacks on Christians, including forced conversions and church burnings. Reports indicate hundreds of incidents annually, with Christians comprising a small but targeted minority. US aid could support legal advocacy for religious freedom and provide humanitarian relief to affected areas. An alliance with India, contingent on protecting Christian rights, could leverage its democratic framework to promote tolerance, aligning with shared values of liberty.

In Syria, the Syrian Civil War and the Islamic State's campaigns displaced over 100,000 Christians, with many fleeing or facing genocide-level persecution. Rebuilding efforts and safe zones for Christians are critical. US aid could prioritize Christian resettlement and infrastructure, while an alliance with Syria's post-conflict government—should it emerge—could ensure minority rights, drawing on America's Christian heritage to foster reconciliation.

Similarly, Christians in Iran, especially converts from Islam, face severe penalties, including execution, under strict Islamic laws. The Church operates covertly, with many believers arrested annually. Aid could support clandestine ministries and human rights campaigns. An alliance with Iran is unlikely under current leadership, but engaging nations with Christian ties (for example, Armenia) to pressure Iran could align with a just war stance against oppression, using diplomacy over force where possible.

CONCLUSION

To enact this vision, the Christian Patriot must integrate just war and aid principles into foreign policy. First, establish a congressional task force to assess persecution levels, ensuring aid targets nations like those above. Second, create a "Christian Freedom Fund" within the foreign aid budget, allocating a percentage—say, 10 percent—to persecuted communities, delivered through trusted partners. Third, negotiate alliance treaties with nations sharing Christian values, such as Poland or Hungary, which emphasize faith in governance, to form a coalition advocating for religious liberty.

Military engagement should follow just war criteria strictly. For instance, intervention in Nigeria against Boko Haram could be justified if it protects innocents and gains international support, but it must also have clear exit strategies to avoid quagmires. Diplomacy must precede force, reflecting Christ's preference for peace (John 16:33). Public discourse should also shift, with churches educating congregations on global persecution, mobilizing prayer and advocacy.

The New Secular Religion may decry "Christian privilege!" Let them. Billions of tax payer monies have been wasted on secular foreign aid in the form of contraception, abortion, and LGBTQ+ "awareness" campaigns. They are a religion, whether they admit it or not, and it is time that majority of Christian Patriots dethrone them and take back our influence for good.

Scripture offers guidance. Isaiah 1:17 calls us to "defend the oppressed," while Romans 12:18 urges peace where possible. The early Church thrived under persecution, suggesting that aid and alliances should strengthen, not abandon, believers. Christian just war theory and an *ordo amoris* favoring suffering Christians under the foot of persecution will guide Christian Patriots to defend the oppressed with moral clarity, while prioritizing foreign aid for persecuted Christians fulfills Christ's compassion. Alliances with nations sharing Christian values can amplify this mission, creating a global witness to God's love. In all nations where Christian blood is spilled in martyrdom, the Church cries out. Will we answer? As stewards of a nation blessed with power, let us act with faith, ensuring our policies reflect the Prince of Peace who calls us to justice and mercy. The task is daunting, but with God, all things are possible (Matthew 19:26).

ACTION ITEMS

1. Teach and defend the Parable of the Good Samaritan and the Augustinian *ordo amoris* as the guide to universal love and "doing good to everyone within reach."
2. Prioritize national aid to assist nations aligned with Christian values and privilege those places where Christians are terrorized, persecuted, and martyred.
3. Investigate and abolish all foreign funding that is contrary to Natural Law and Christian social teaching. No more foreign funding for sexual degeneracy, unjust conflict, or wasteful projects.

STRATEGY 12

SLAVERY AS DEBT, TAXES, AND INFLATION

As I arranged the chapters of this book, I debated on whether to include a chapter on finances, money, and economics. Then I recalled a sermon I once heard stating that our Lord Jesus Christ spoke more often about money than He did about so many other important subjects.

- Kingdom of God/Heaven: 62
- Money, Wealth, and Possessions: 33
- Sin, Repentance, and Forgiveness: 28
- Love/Compassion: 25
- Faith/Belief: 24
- Judgment/End Times: 21
- Prayer/Relationship with God: 19
- Discipleship: 18
- Hypocrisy: 15
- Hell: 15
- Humility/Service: 14

A simple word count does not reflect a proper hierarchy of topics in the teachings of Christ. Nevertheless, Jesus Christ dedicated a significant portion of His teaching ministry to addressing the human struggle of balancing money and serving God. As Christ says, "No man can serve two masters. For either he will hate the one and love the other, or he will sustain the one and despise the other. You cannot serve God and mammon" (Matthew 6:24). The Old Testament book of Proverbs is also a treasure trove of wise advice on money, detachment, and lending.

The global economy pulses with innovation and ambition. Yet beneath its sheen lies a system often at odds with Christian principles—usury enslaves, materialism reigns, and families falter under financial strain. Scripture calls us to a higher standard: "Seek first the kingdom of God and his righteousness, and all these things will be added to you" (Matthew 6:33). From the early church of the catacombs to our post-industrial, digital cloud economy, Christians have wrestled with how to order economic life justly. Saint Augustine taught that "the measure of love is to love without measure," yet this love must be rightly ordered (*City of God,* 19.14). Mindful that Jesus Christ overturned the tables of exploitative money-changers (John 2:15), this chapter proposes transformative suggestions for the Christian Patriot to align the economy with Christian ethics, redeeming it for God's glory.

THE DANGERS OF DEBT AND SIN OF USURY

Every Christian should memorize the proverb: "The rich rules over the poor, and the borrower is the slave of the lender" (Proverbs 22:7). Today, young people are so straddled with debt—college debt, credit card debt, medical debt, and property debt—that it becomes difficult for them to marry and start families. Before the Reformation in the 1500s, Christian culture was united against the dangers of debt and usury. Debt, which is so pervasive in modern economies, carries profound dangers that the Christian Bible repeatedly warns against. From the slavery it imposes to the spiritual bondage it fosters, Sacred Scripture presents debt as a threat to God's design for human flourishing. Proverbs 22:7 reminds us that "the borrower is the slave of the lender." This foundational verse frames debt not as neutral but as a power dynamic that enslaves, stripping away freedom and dignity. For Christians, this is no mere economic concern—it's a spiritual peril that distances us from reliance on God.

The Old Testament sets a clear tone. Deuteronomy 15:1–2 mandates a sabbatical release of debts every seven years, signaling God's intent to prevent perpetual bondage: "Every creditor shall release what he has lent to his neighbor." This wasn't optional—debt's accumulation was a distortion of community, risking exploitation. Exodus 22:25 reinforces this, forbidding interest on loans to the poor: "You shall not exact interest from him." Usury, the profit from lending, was an abomination because it preyed on vulnerability, a theme echoed by Nehemiah's outrage at his people's debt slavery: "We are forcing our sons and daughters to be slaves" (Nehemiah 5:5). These laws reveal debt's danger: it hardens hearts and fractures God's covenant people.

Our Lord Jesus Christ amplifies this in the New Testament, intertwining debt with spiritual stakes. In Matthew 6:24, He warns, "You cannot serve God and mammon," linking financial entanglements to idolatry. Debt, as a form of mammon, competes with God for allegiance, chaining the borrower to worldly masters. The parable of the unforgiving servant (Matthew 18:23–35) illustrates this further—a servant forgiven a massive debt (10,000 talents, billions today) refuses mercy to another, showing how debt can corrupt character. Jesus' call to settle debts quickly—"lest you be put in prison...until you have paid the last penny" (Matthew 5:25–26)—

underscores its urgency, both practically and as a metaphor for unresolved sin.

The Bible's warnings aren't abstract. Proverbs 22:26–27 cautions, "Be not one of those who give pledges.... If you have nothing with which to pay, why should your bed be taken from under you?" Debt risks losing essentials—home, security, peace—echoing modern crises where US consumer debt hit $17.5 trillion in 2023. St. Paul adds a radical edge: "Owe no one anything, except to love each other" (Romans 13:8). Debt-free living aligns with love, while borrowing fosters dependence on lenders over God.

The danger, then, is threefold: debt enslaves physically, tempts spiritually, and destabilizes society morally. Augustine saw rightly ordered love as prioritizing God (*City of God*, 19.14); debt disorders this, tethering us to mammon and the cycle of compounding interest. Christians are called to trust God's provision—"Give us this day our daily bread" (Matthew 6:11)—not lenders' chains. In a debt-soaked culture, Scripture's clarion call is liberation through faith, not bondage through borrowing.

COLLEGE DEBT AND PERSONAL DEBT?

How, then, do Christians move forward in an economy built on credit and debt? Mortgages for homes are hard to avoid. Yet other forms of debt should be avoided and we should help our children and young people to avoid mistakes early in life. The presumption that everyone should attend college and rack up debt doing so is ludicrous. A four-year college degree is beneficial, but a majority of college grads confess that they don't actually use their degree in their current line of work. Certainly, doctors, lawyers, and professors require college education and advanced degrees. However, is going to college *for the sake of college* a proper Christian perspective for building our future—to say nothing of the woke, liberal agenda promoted in college classrooms?

Christians are also returning to the trades and encouraging our children to attend trade schools or internships to learn valuable, high-paying skills. I have met many young men serving as electricians, plumbers, welders, renovators, and builders. who enjoy salaries two to three times higher than recent college graduates. They learn a skill, excel at their craft, create LLCs, hire laborers, and build successful companies. They can accomplish this without college degrees.

Beyond avoiding college debt (which is not possible for everyone), we must return to frugality and living within our means. The advent of Instagram creates a fake environment of false status based on exotic vacations, fancy restaurants, new luxury cars, new designer clothes, and high-end experiences. We must teach ourselves and our children that these things, Christ tells us, do *not make us happy*. In the quest to keep up with the online Joneses, people are tempted to buy on credit, max out credit cards, and repeatedly refinance their home to buy the cars, boats, trips, and clothes that will make them feel as if they *made it*. However, it is never enough. Mammon is an unforgiving "god."

For those already in debt, the incentive should be on getting out of debt. The deeper in debt we are, the deeper in slavery we become. This must be ingrained in our children. It's much better to drive an older car, live in a home that matches our income, and eat and travel within our budget. When we emerge from debt, we are empowered to save, invest, and build active and passive income to raise our standards of life and bless others in need.

ABOLISH USURY IN LENDING

So far, we have discussed the personal danger of debt. We must turn to the societal danger that debt places on us as a nation. Usury—excessive interest on loans—contradicts biblical mandates. Exodus 22:25 instructs, "If you lend money to any of my people with you who is poor, you shall not be like a moneylender to him, and you shall not exact interest from him." Recently, US consumer debt hit $18 trillion, per the Federal Reserve, much of it laden with interest rates exceeding 20 percent on credit cards.[1] Aquinas condemned usury as "unjust gain" (*Summa Theologiae*, II-II, Q. 78, A. 1), arguing money's purpose is exchange, not profit through time.

During his 2024 campaign, Trump proposed a temporary cap on credit card interest rates at 10 percent, a significant reduction from the 2024 average of 21.5 percent (Bankrate data). He articulated this on September 18, 2024, at a rally in Uniondale, New York, stating, "While working Americans catch up, we're going to put a temporary cap on credit card interest rates...around 10 percent. We can't let them make 25 and 30 percent." This pledge aimed to alleviate the burden of record-high credit card debt, which reached $1.14 trillion in Q2 2024 (*New York Fed*), amid rising delinquencies (9.1 percent of balances).

Since Trump's inauguration on January 20, 2025, the policy has gained momentum through legislative allies. On February 4, 2025, Senator Bernie Sanders (I-VT) and Christian Senator Josh Hawley (R-MO) introduced the "10 Percent Credit Card Interest Rate Cap Act," a bill that directly reflects Trump's campaign promise. The legislation, which aims to amend the 1968 Truth in Lending Act, proposes a five-year cap at 10 percent, with Sanders and Hawley leveraging Trump's support to press Congress. Hawley stated, "Capping credit card interest rates at 10 percent, just like President Trump campaigned on, is a straightforward way to provide meaningful relief to working people" (CNBC, February 7, 2025). This bipartisan effort implies the administration is at least tacitly endorsing the initiative, though Trump has not publicly reaffirmed the pledge since taking office. The chief negative to this policy is that capping rates would prevent people with extremely low credit scores from receiving loans—but that is not a bad thing. There is nothing righteous about strapping the poorest of the poor (with abysmal credit ratings) with predatory loans at 20–30 percent!

PROMOTING HOME OWNERSHIP AS A COVENANT

Home ownership, a cornerstone of stability, has slipped—67 percent of Americans owned homes in 2024, down from 69.2 percent in 2004 (US Census Bureau). Going back, Adam and Eve and down through history, owning land and owning a home were integral for the growth of families and their security over time. Land and houses often passed from generation to generation over centuries.

The chief reasons for the decline in home ownership are inflation and the erosion of the dollar. Let us compare the price of a house relative to annual salary in 1950 as opposed to today:

1950: Houses Relative to Annual Salary

- Average House Price: Approximately $7,354 (US Census Bureau).
- Average Annual Salary: Around $3,300 for a household (US Census Bureau).
- House Price-to-Income Ratio: Dividing $7,354 by $3,300 yields approximately **2.23 years of annual salary.**

In 1950, it took a man 2.23 years on an average salary to buy an average house. Now, let's compare this to today's numbers.

2025: Projected Houses Relative to Annual Salary

- Average House Price: Approximately $433,100 (National Association of Realtors).
- Average Annual Salary: The median household income in 2023 was $74,580 (US Census Bureau).
- House Price-to-Income Ratio: Dividing $467,000 by $81,300 yields approximately **5.74 years of annual salary.**

In 2025, it takes a man 5.74 years on an average salary to buy an average house. Comparing 1950 to 2015, an average house today is over twice as expensive (2.57x) in terms of salary.

In 1950, a worker could own a home outright in under three years, embodying biblical provision. By 2025, it's a six-year slog, often with thirty-year mortgages, binding families to lenders. A Christian response might advocate policies—like the Amish model of community loans or rate caps—to restore balance, ensuring homes remain a blessing, not a burden. However, the reason for this increasingly impossible spread between wages and home prices has to do with inflation and immigration. Inflation devalues the currency. Immigration increases demand for homes (causing prices to increase) and brings in more competition for labor (causing wages to decrease). It is a perfect storm. Let's examine each factor.

ENDING THE FEDERAL RESERVE

The Federal Reserve, established in 1913, manipulates currency through debt-based money—$35 trillion national debt in 2024—echoing Proverbs 11:1, "A false balance is an abomination to the Lord." Since the currency is no longer backed with gold and silver, it is at the whims of the powerful elite and international bankers. The dirty secret is that these predators prefer to debase the currency because it increases the value of their assets (banks, real estate corporations), which also makes it easier to pay off loans and lower rates with loan balances that become easier to pay with time. The game of the Federal Reserve assists the richest who watch their assets swell, but it hurts the middle class and poor who are trying to fill the gap between their wages and the ever-increasing price of goods, groceries, gas, cars, and houses.

Christians must become savvy enough to understand that the Federal Reserve is a rigged game—much like trying to win at the slots in a casino. The house always wins. We must coalesce, abolish the Fed, and return to a gold-backed dollar, capped at $50 billion in circulation, based on 1890s levels adjusted for population. We must establish a Treasury-managed system that prioritizes stability over inflation, consistent with biblical honesty in weights and measures (Leviticus 19:36). This limits the tyranny of debt, though transition risks require careful phasing.

IMMIGRATION AND WAGE GAPS

Immigration, a divisive issue in the United States, carries economic consequences that challenge citizens' livelihoods, particularly through wage suppression. For the Christian Patriot, this tension pits stewardship of one's community against the call to love the stranger, revealing a complex interplay of justice and mercy. Scripture commands, "You shall not oppress a sojourner" (Exodus 23:9), yet also urges care for one's own: "If anyone does not provide for his relatives, and especially for members of his household, he has denied the faith" (1 Timothy 5:8). Uncontrolled immigration, especially illegal inflows, often hurts wages for American citizens, a reality that demands attention through a biblical lens of fairness and provision.

Economically, immigration increases labor supply, which can depress wages, particularly for low-skilled workers. In 2023, the US had 11 million undocumented immigrants (Pew Research Center), many competing in sectors like construction, agriculture, and hospitality—jobs held by 22 million native-born workers without college degrees (Bureau of Labor Statistics, BLS). A 2024 George Borjas study found that a 10 percent increase in immigrant labor reduces native wages by 3–4 percent in these fields. For example, construction wages, averaging $35,000 annually (BLS 2023), stagnated despite demand, as employers hired undocumented workers at $10–$15 hourly versus $20 for citizens. This aligns with the Congressional Budget Office's 2024 estimate: immigration lowered wages for the bottom 20 percent of earners by 2 percent over a decade.[2]

In case you are tempted to think that immigrating workers only affect lower-paying jobs, estimates from the Economic Policy Institute (EPI, 2023) peg the immigrant H-1B workforce at approximately 600,000 workers in the United States. There are estimated to be an additional 130,000 new H-1B workers every year. Pew Research notes that 73 percent are from India, mostly in computer-related jobs (65 percent, median salary $123,600). Tech giants like Amazon lead the way with 11,000 immigrant H-1B approvals. Immigration is not just affecting day labor jobs. It is creeping into the tech sector and pushing out native workers. Just as we protest factories closing down and moving to foreign countries for cheaper labor and nonexistent tariffs, so we must also protest the influx of labor from other nations. The dirty secret of H-1B tech jobs for immigrants is that since they are dependent on their jobs to remain in the USA, they often settle for lower pay and longer hours. Once again, it is a ploy of corporations to enrich themselves while taking advantage of their fellow citizens and immigrants.

From a Christian perspective, uncontrolled immigration hurts the native working-class citizens struggling to fulfill Proverbs 13:22:

"The good man leaveth heirs, sons, and grandsons: and the substance of the sinner is kept for the just." Wages stagnated—median household income rose only 3 percent to $74,580 from 2019 to 2023 (Census)—while housing costs soared ($467,000 projected for 2025, NAR) and trapped families in debt. The politicians and corporations fighting for increased immigration often prioritize profit over people by exploiting cheap labor, which echoes James 5:4: "The wages of the laborers...which you kept back by fraud, are crying out against you." Immigration's wage pressure thus undermines God's design for work's dignity (Colossians 3:23). We cannot expect the next generation to build healthy, stable families if the prices of groceries and houses are soaring on the wings of inflation while wages drop with the influx of immigrants.

INCENTIVIZING BIRTH RATES WITH ECONOMIC SUPPORT

In a previous chapter, we discussed the need to lift our birth rate. The US birth rate hit a record low of 1.62 children per woman in 2023 (CDC), below the replacement rate of 2.1, which threatens future prosperity. Genesis 1:28 commands, "Be fruitful and multiply," and "Children are a heritage from the Lord." Given our challenging economic landscape, Christian Patriots might rally behind a $10,000 tax-free grant for each child born, increasing with each additional birth (e.g., $15,000 for the second), funded by reallocating $5 billion from corporate tax breaks or by tariffs levied on imports from other nations. Pair this with free maternal healthcare, reflecting the Christian reverence for life and countering Malthusian fears with faith in God's provision.

SIMPLIFY OR ABOLISH INCOME TAX

Taxation is another heavy burden on the citizen class and hampers our economic freedom. The US income tax system, with its 73,954-page code, places a burden on citizens while favoring the wealthy—the top 1 percent paid 45.8 percent of taxes yet held 31.9 percent of wealth (Federal Reserve, 2023). A straightforward solution that Christian Patriots may unify around to replace the progressive tax system with a flat one is a 10 percent income tithe above a $30,000 exemption, mirroring the Old Testament tithe. If God didn't ask for more than 10 percent, why should Uncle Sam demand more?

Ultimately, the abolition of income tax should be kept in our sights. The American income tax's origins trace back to the Civil War. In 1861, Congress passed the Revenue Act, imposing a 3 percent tax on incomes over $800 (about $27,000 today) to fund the Union effort, raising $55 million by 1866. This temporary measure lapsed in 1872. A second attempt in 1894, a 2 percent tax on incomes over $4,000, was struck down by the Supreme Court in *Pollock v. Farmers' Loan & Trust Co.* (1895) as unconstitutional, affirming limits on federal power. Regretfully, the Progressive Era's push for wealth redistribution birthed the 16th Amendment, ratified February 3, 1913, granting Congress authority to tax incomes "from whatever source derived." The Revenue Act of 1913 followed, levying 1 percent on incomes above $3,000 (plus surtaxes up to 6 percent), initially affecting only 1 percent of Americans. By 2023, it ballooned to $2.2 trillion annually.

For Christian Patriots, this draconian evolution in taxation is troubling. Scripture frames wealth as God's gift for stewardship, not state seizure—"The earth is the Lord's and the fullness thereof" (Psalm 23:1). The income tax, with its progressive rates (currently a 37 percent top bracket), greatly exceeds Pharaoh's oppressive 20 percent grain tax (Genesis 47:24), which *enslaved* Israel. The tax's complexity—costing $409 billion in compliance annually (Tax Foundation, 2023)—violates Proverbs 11:1: "A false balance is an abomination to the Lord." It punishes labor (Colossians 3:23: "Work heartily, as for the Lord") while favoring loopholes for the rich, who pay 45.8 percent of taxes but hold 31.9 percent of wealth (Federal Reserve, 2023). Taxation is a game with rules too complicated for the average person to navigate. The proliferation of regulations makes it fair game for corporations and the wealthy to hire teams of lawyers and tax experts to manipulate the system. Meanwhile, the hardworking middle class is left behind. Moreover, consider this: If you pay 33 percent in taxes (most people do), then you are effectively working one-third of the year for the government. The wages you earn during those four months go directly to the government. You work four months each year, not for yourself, but for the government—who often squanders that money. When viewed from the perspective of working January, February, March, and April of each year for the government, the only proper conclusion is that we are slaves to the government. It must end.

CONCLUSION

A Christian economy isn't utopian—it's a return to biblical roots, where justice, mercy, and humility (Micah 6:8) guide markets, trade, and human interactions. Usury gives way to fairness, debt transforms into freedom, and greed is replaced by generosity. These steps, along with those outlined in the previous eleven chapters—rooted in Scripture and theology—provide a blueprint to redeem commerce, not just for profit, but for God's people and His glory. The journey requires sacrifice, but, as Jesus promises, "For he that will save his life, shall lose it: and he that shall lose his life for my sake, shall find it." (Matthew 16:25). Let us begin.

ACTION ITEMS

1. Educate Christians and young people about the danger of debt and the slavery it creates.
2. Identify usury as sinful and dangerous—particularly to the vulnerable and poor.
3. Teach about the dangers of materialism and keeping up with the Joneses. Things do not make you happy.
4. Aid in home ownership.
5. Control immigration and work visas to prioritize the native worker.
6. Reduce income tax to a 10 percent flat tax or abolish it altogether.

SERVING THE CITY OF GOD, LIVING IN THE CITY OF MAN

As we reach the culmination of *Christian Patriot: 12 Steps to Creating One Nation Under God,* we stand at a crossroads of faith and nationhood. The New Secular Religion is growing and making inroads. It is taking ground, and we often feel like we are retreating. Let the Christian Patriot stand his ground. Onward, Christian soldiers. Fill the vacuum with the prayer, sacrifice, patience, and the cross of Christ as our standard. The separation of church and state does not separate our Christian belief from patriotic commitment to our country. There is no separation within our hearts.

The journey through these twelve steps—rooted in Scripture, prayer, and action—has revealed a vision for nationhood where Christians, living in Augustine's City of Man, serve the eternal City of God with unwavering devotion. Saint Augustine taught us that these two cities coexist: the City of Man, bound by earthly desires and temporal power, and the City of God, defined by love for the Lord and His eternal kingdom. However, these two cities are linked by the presence of Christians: "For where there are two or three gathered together in my name, there am I in the midst of them" (Matthew 18:20).

For American Christian Patriots, we dwell in America—a nation flawed yet blessed with a Christian heritage—while our ultimate allegiance lies with God's kingdom. This conclusion affirms America's

Christian identity, explores how believers can transform its culture and politics, and calls us to rise as agents of renewal, making our nation truly "one nation under God." America's roots are undeniably Christian, a truth etched in its founding and sustained by its people. From the original colonies claiming to be "a city upon a hill" (Matthew 5:14) to the Declaration of Independence's appeal to "the Laws of Nature and of Nature's God" in 1776, a Christian pulse has vivified this land.

Today, with 2.66 billion Christians worldwide and 63 percent of Americans identifying as Christian, we have the numbers, but we need mobilization. We must follow practical steps, and I hope this book presents prudent and inspired steps to achieve our goal of one nation under God. As Psalm 33:12 reminds us, "Blessed is the nation whose God is the Lord." All it takes for evil to prevail is for the good men to do nothing. The New Secular Religion is at the gates. Degeneracy, abortion, pornography, divorce, human trafficking, immoral wars, materialism, and identity confusion are their tools for darkness. Jesus Christ said that we are the light of the world and the salt of the earth. Are we filling our lives, families, and culture with that light and salt?

Augustine's dual-city paradigm offers us a compass as we orient this strange terrain. This tension is not paralysis but purpose. Augustine argued that Christians, while in the City of Man, must use its goods for divine ends. This means evangelizing culture and engaging in politics—not retreating into our private conscience but shining as light. The City of Man is not our enemy to destroy but our mission field to redeem. As Christian Patriots, we steward this nation, trusting God's promise: "If my people who are called by my name humble themselves, and pray, then I will hear from heaven... and heal their land" (2 Chronicles 7:14).

I leave you with these twelve steps as a final strategy and challenge you to pick three of them to implement over the next twelve months:

1. Evangelize your soul, family, and culture.
2. Take up public space with Christian signs, monuments, crosses, and Scripture verses, and honor Christian holidays and Sundays.
3. Define matrimony according to God's definition and insist on it in your sphere of influence.
4. Embrace traditional family and the call to bear and educate children in the Lord as first fruits offered to Christ.
5. End abortion with compassion and conviction through teaching, pregnancy ministry, and political influence.
6. Equip your children, grandchildren, or children at your church with Christian education and work for Christian schools and homeschoolers to thrive.
7. Educate and influence society to defend parental rights over their children.
8. Abolish pornography and make it illegal.
9. Educate others on human trafficking and advocate for national investigations against human trafficking within and on our borders.
10. Educate others on just war theory and vote against candidates who seek wars for the sake of gain or for unlawful cause.
11. Bring awareness to government waste in the realm of foreign aid and advocate for more aid to Christian allies and to places where Christians are persecuted and martyred.
12. Eschew materialism and keeping up with the Joneses. Be content with what we have and teach the dangers of debt. Socially, fight against predatory interest rates and work

against fiat currencies and central banks that manipulate the currency for the benefit of billionaires.

Our goals are as high as heaven, but that is where Christ is seated. Christ is our Lord. Christ is our Savior. Christ is our King. Christ is our Shepherd. As our Good Shepherd, He knows what we need and where He needs to lead us. If you take away anything from this book, embrace Strategy 1: Christ in the Soul. All social and political action is corrupted and wasted if Christ is not the center of that activity. Christian Patriots, may God richly bless you. I'll see you on the battlefield, and, God willing, in our everlasting City of God.

> "You are the salt of the earth, but if salt has lost its taste, how shall its saltiness be restored? It is no longer good for anything except to be thrown out and trampled under people's feet. You are the light of the world. A city set on a hill cannot be hidden" (Matthew 5:13).

You are the light of the world and the salt of the earth...so go out there and be salty.

Thank you for reading *Christian Patriot.* I hope you were edified and inspired to transform our world and nations for Jesus Christ. May I ask a couple of favors from you? First, would you please say a prayer for me and my family? Secondly, if you found this book helpful or inspirational, would you please take a moment to review *Christian Patriot* on Amazon.com or Goodreads.com? I would be especially grateful. I am thankful for your support and prayers.

In Christ,
Taylor R. Marshall

BIBLIOGRAPHY

Adams, John. *Diary*, February 22, 1756. In *The Works of John Adams*, edited by Charles Francis Adams, vol. 2, 3–4. Boston: Little, Brown, 1850.

Adams, John. *Diary*, July 26, 1796. In *The Works of John Adams*, edited by Charles Francis Adams, vol. 3, 410–411. Boston: Little, Brown, 1851.

Adams, John. *Letter to Abigail Adams*, undated. In *Familiar Letters of John Adams and His Wife Abigail Adams, During the Revolution*, edited by Charles Francis Adams, 123–124. New York: Hurd and Houghton, 1876.

Adams, John. *Letter to the Officers of the First Brigade of the Third Division of the Militia of Massachusetts*, October 11, 1798. In *Revolutionary Services and Civil Life of General William Hull*, by Maria Campbell and James Freeman Clarke, 265–266. New York: D. Appleton, 1848.

Adams, John. *Letter to Thomas Jefferson*, December 25, 1813. In *The Adams-Jefferson Letters: The Complete Correspondence Between Thomas Jefferson and Abigail and John Adams*, edited by Lester J. Cappon, 386–388. Chapel Hill: University of North Carolina Press, 1959.

Aquinas, Thomas. *Summa Theologiae*. Translated by Fathers of the English Dominican Province. 5 vols. New York: Benziger Bros., 1947.

Aristotle. *Politics*. Translated by Benjamin Jowett. Mineola, NY: Dover Publications, 2000.

Armas, K. (2025, January 31). JD Vance is wrong: Jesus doesn't ask us to rank our love for others. National Catholic Reporter. https://www.ncronline.org/opinion/guest-voices/jd-vance-wrong-jesus-doesnt-ask-us-rank-our-love-others

Augustine. *The City of God*. Translated by Henry Bettenson. London: Penguin Classics, 2003.

Augustine. *Letter 138 to Marcellinus*, ca. 412. In *The Works of Saint Augustine: A Translation for the 21st Century*. Translated by Edmund Hill, vol. 2, Letters 100–155, 209–210. Hyde Park, NY: New City Press, 2002.

Augustine. *De Magistro* (On the Teacher). Translated by Peter King. Indianapolis: Hackett Publishing, 1995.

"Le Joueur généreux" [The Generous Gambler]. In *Le Spleen de Paris: Petits poèmes en prose,* 85–89, 1864. Paris: Michel Lévy Frères, 1869.

Bavinck, Herman. *Reformed Dogmatics, Vol. 3, Sin and Salvation in Christ*. Translated by John Vriend, edited by John Bolt. Grand Rapids, MI: Baker Academic, 2006.

Bonhoeffer, Dietrich. *Ethics*. Translated by Reinhard Krauss and Charles C. West. Minneapolis: Fortress Press, 2005. First published 1949.

Chesterton, G.K. *The Superstition of Divorce*. London: Chatto & Windus, 1920.

Codex Theodosianus. Edited by Theodor Mommsen and Paul M. Meyer. 3 vols. Berlin: Weidmann, 1905. Cited sections include 3.5.1; 3.7.2; 3.13; 9.7.3; 9.24.1.

Dobson, James C. Interview with Ted Bundy, January 23, 1989. In *Fatal Addiction: Ted Bundy's Final Interview*. Colorado Springs, CO: Focus on the Family, 1989. Transcript and audio archived at https://www.focusonthefamily.com/media/ted-bundy-interview (accessed March 11, 2025).

Dvorchak, Robert J., and Lisa Holewa, eds. *The Milwaukee Cannibal: Jeffrey Dahmer's Confessions.* New York: Dell Publishing, 1997. Contains transcript of *Jeffrey Dahmer: The Exclusive Interview,* aired February 17, 1993, 143–148.

Eusebius. *Ecclesiastical History and Life of Constantine.* Translated by Philip Schaff and Henry Wace. In *Nicene and Post-Nicene Fathers,* Second Series, vol. 1. New York: Christian Literature Publishing Co., 1890.

Guttmacher Institute. "Monthly Abortion Provision Study: Preliminary Findings—Abortion Incidence in the United States, 2023." Guttmacher Institute, 2023. https://www.guttmacher.org/monthly-abortion-provision-study.

James, M.R., trans. *The Apocalypse of Peter.* In *The Apocryphal New Testament: Being the Apocryphal Gospels, Acts, Epistles, and Apocalypses, with Other Narratives and Fragments,* 505–521. Oxford: Clarendon Press, 1924.

Jefferson, Thomas. Letter to John Adams, October 13, 1813. In *The Adams-Jefferson Letters: The Complete Correspondence Between Thomas Jefferson and Abigail and John Adams,* edited by Lester J. Cappon, 383–386. Chapel Hill: University of North Carolina Press, 1959.

Jordan, James B. *The Law of the Covenant: An Exposition of Exodus 21–23.* Tyler, TX: Institute for Christian Economics, 1984.

Kennedy, John F. "Inaugural Address, January 20, 1961." In *Public Papers of the Presidents of the United States: John F. Kennedy, 1961, 1–3.* Washington, DC: Government Printing Office, 1962. Also available at American Presidency Project, https://www.presidency.ucsb.edu/documents/inaugural-address-2.

Laats, Adam. "Our Schools, Our Country: American Evangelicals, Public Schools, and the Supreme Court Decisions of 1962 and 1963." *Journal of Religious History 36*, no. 3 (2012): 319–334.

Lewis, C.S. *The Four Loves*. London: Geoffrey Bles, 1960.

Lewis, C.S. *The Screwtape Letters*. London: Geoffrey Bles, 1942.

Lincoln, Abraham. "Second Inaugural Address, March 4, 1865." In *The Collected Works of Abraham Lincoln*, edited by Roy P. Basler, vol. 8, 332–333. New Brunswick, NJ: Rutgers University Press, 1953. Also available at National Archives, https://www.archives.gov/exhibits/american_originals/inaug2.html.

Lunde, Donald T. *The Die Song: A Journey into the Mind of a Mass Murderer*. San Francisco: San Francisco Book Co., 1991.

Lutz, Donald S. *The Origins of American Constitutionalism*. Baton Rouge: Louisiana State University Press, 1988.

MacKinnon, Catharine A. "Pornography as Trafficking." *Michigan Journal of International Law* 26, no. 4 (2005): 993–1012. https://repository.law.umich.edu/mjil/vol26/iss4/1.

Marshall, Taylor R. *The Eternal City: Rome and the Origins of Catholic Christianity*. Dallas: Saint John Press, 2012.

New York Times. "Barack Obama's 'Bitter' Comments." April 11, 2008. https://www.nytimes.com/2008/04/11/us/politics/11obama.html.

Norris, Joel. *Arthur Shawcross: The Genesee River Killer*. New York: Pinnacle Books, 1992.

Office of Inspector General. "ICE Cannot Monitor All Unaccompanied Migrant Children Released from DHS and HHS Custody." OIG-24-30. Washington, DC: Department of Homeland Security, 2024.

Plato. *Laws*. Translated by Benjamin Jowett. In *The Dialogues of Plato*, vol. 4. Oxford: Clarendon Press, 1871.

Plato. *Republic.* Translated by Benjamin Jowett. In *The Dialogues of Plato,* vol. 3. Oxford: Clarendon Press, 1871.

Pope John Paul II. *Familiaris Consortio.* Vatican City: Libreria Editrice Vaticana, 1981.

Pope Leo XIII. *Rerum Novarum.* In *Acta Sanctae Sedis* 23 (1890–1891): 641–670.

Pope Pius XI. *Quadragesimo Anno.* In *Acta Apostolicae Sedis* 22 (1930): 529–548.

Texas Public Policy Foundation. "Busting the 'No Money' Myth." October 2, 2023. https://www.texaspolicy.com/busting-the-no-money/.

Thompson, Krissah. "For Decades They Hid Jefferson's Relationship with Her. Now Monticello Is Making Room for Sally Hemings." *The Washington Post,* February 18, 2017. https://www.washingtonpost.com/news/post-nation/wp/2017/02/18/for-decades-they-hid-jeffersons-mistress-now-monticello-is-making-room-for-sally-hemings/.

Washington, George. Letter to the Delaware Indian Chiefs, May 12, 1779. In *The Writings of George Washington,* edited by John C. Fitzpatrick, vol. 15, 55–56. Washington, DC: US Government Printing Office, 1932.

ENDNOTES

Chapter 1

1. "Barack Obama's 'Bitter' Comments," *The New York Times, April 11, 2008, https://www.nytimes.com/2008/04/11/us/politics/11obama.html.*
2. C.S. Lewis, *The Screwtape Letters, Letter 7. London: Geoffrey Bles, 1942.*
3. Charles Pierre Baudelaire, "La plus belle des ruses du diable est de vous persuader qu'il n'existe pas," in *The Generous Gambler* (*Le Joueur généreux, 1864*).

Chapter 2

1. Thomas Aquinas, *Summa Theologiae II-II, Q. 101, A. 1.*
2. Thomas Aquinas, *Summa Theologiae II-II, Q. 101, A. 1.*

Chapter 3

1. Adam Laats, "Our Schools, Our Country: American Evangelicals, Public Schools, and the Supreme Court Decisions of 1962 and 1963," *Journal of Religious History, 36.3* (*2012*)*: 319–334 at p. 321–22.*
2. George Washington, *Letter to the Delaware Indian Chiefs, May 12, 1779, in The Writings of George Washington, vol. 15, ed. John C. Fitzpatrick* (*Washington, DC: US Government Printing Office, 1932*)*, 55–56.*
3. Abraham Lincoln, *Second Inaugural Address, March 4, 1865, National Archives, https://www.loc.gov/resource/lprbscsm.scsm0304.*
4. John F. Kennedy, *Inaugural Address, January 20, 1961, The American Presidency Project, https://www.presidency.ucsb.edu/node/80437.*
5. Adam Laats, "Our Schools, Our Country: American Evangelicals, Public Schools, and the Supreme Court Decisions of 1962 and 1963," *Journal of Religious History, 36, no. 3* (*2012*)*: 321–22.*
6. Thomas Jefferson to John Adams, October 13, 1813, in *The Adams-Jefferson Letters: The Complete Correspondence Between Thomas Jefferson and Abigail and John Adams, ed. Lester J. Cappon* (*Chapel Hill: University of North Carolina Press, 1959*)*, 385.*

7. Krissah Thompson, "For Decades They Hid Jefferson's Relationship with Her. Now Monticello Is Making Room for Sally Hemings," *The Washington Post, February 18, 2017, archived from the original on February 27, 2018, retrieved January 30, 2025, https://www.washingtonpost.com/lifestyle/style/for-decades-they-hid-jeffersons-mistress-now-monticello-is-making-room-for-sally-hemings/2017/02/18/d410d660-f222-11e6-8d72-263470bf0401_story.html.*
8. John Adams to Thomas Jefferson, December 25, 1813, in *The Adams-Jefferson Letters, ed. Lester J. Cappon (Chapel Hill: University of North Carolina Press, 1959).*
9. Donald Lutz, *The Origins of American Constitutionalism (Baton Rouge: Louisiana* State University Press, 1988).
10. John Adams, *Letter to the Officers of the First Brigade of the Third Division of the Militia of Massachusetts, October 11, 1798, in Revolutionary Services and Civil Life of General William Hull (New York: 1848), 265–66. There are some differences in the version that appeared in The Works of John Adams (Boston: 1854), 9:228–29, most notably the words "or gallantry" instead of "and licentiousness."*
11. John Adams, *Diary, February 22, 1756, in The Adams-Jefferson Letters: The Complete Correspondence Between Thomas Jefferson and Abigail and John Adams, edited by Lester J. Cappon (Chapel Hill: University of North Carolina Press, 1959), 383.*
12. John Adams, *Diary, July 26, 1796, in The Adams-Jefferson Letters: The Complete Correspondence Between Thomas Jefferson and Abigail and John Adams, edited by Lester J. Cappon (Chapel Hill: University of North Carolina Press, 1959), 506.*

Chapter 4

1. C.S. Lewis, *The Four Loves (1960), 58.*
2. Pope Leo XIII, "Rerum Novarum," *Acta Sanctae Sedis, vol. 23 (1890–91): 645, para. 12.*
3. Pope Pius XI, "Casti Connubii," *Acta Apostolicae Sedis, vol. 22 (1930): 540, para. 10.*
4. Dietrich Bonhoeffer, *Ethics* (1949), 288.
5. G.K. Chesterton, *The Superstition of Divorce (1920), chap. 1.*
6. Augustine, *The City of God, book 19, chap. 15.*
7. Thomas Aquinas, *Summa Theologiae II-II, Q. 64, A. 3.*
8. Herman Bavinck, *Reformed Dogmatics, vol. 3, 219.*
9. James Jordan, *The Law of the Covenant* (1984), 45.
10. Thomas Aquinas, *Summa Theologiae* I-II, Q. 94, A. 2.
11. Thomas Aquinas, *Summa Theologiae* I-II, Q. 91, A. 2: "The Natural Law is nothing else than the rational creature's participation in the eternal law."
12. Thomas Aquinas, *Summa Theologiae I-II, Q. 96, A. 4.*
13. Thomas Aquinas, *Summa Theologiae I-II, Q. 90, A. 4.*

Chapter 5

1. Taylor R. Marshall, *The Eternal City: Rome and the Origins of Catholic Christianity* (Saint John Press, 2012).
2. Eusebius, *Ecclesiastical History, book 5, and Life of Constantine.*

Strategy 3

1. John Adams, Letters to Abigail Adams.
2. Aristotle, *Politics*, trans. Benjamin Jowett (Mineola, NY: Dover Publications, 2000).
3. Codex Theodosianus, 3.5.1
4. Codex Theodosianus, 9.7.3.
5. Codex Theodosianus, 3.7.2.
6. Codex Theodosianus, 3.13.
7. Codex Theodosianus, 9.24.1.
8. John Paul II, *Letter to Families (1994), where he states in section 13.*
9. Plato, *Laws, Book 8.*

Strategy 5

1. Guttmacher Institute. (2023). "Monthly Abortion Provision Study: Preliminary findings—Abortion incidence in the United States, 2023," https://www.guttmacher.org/monthly-abortion-provision-study.
2. New International Version translation.
3. M. R. James, trans., *The Apocalypse of Peter*, in *The Apocryphal New Testament: Being the Apocryphal Gospels, Acts, Epistles, and Apocalypses, with Other Narratives and Fragments*, 505–521 (Oxford: Clarendon Press, 1924).
4. Heartbeat International, "About Heartbeat International," accessed June 3, 2025, https://www.heartbeatinternational.org/about; Andrea Trudden, "10 Numbers You Should Know About Pregnancy Centers," Pregnancy Help News, December 19, 2017, https://pregnancyhelpnews.com/10-numbers-you-should-know-about-pregnancy-centers.[](https://pregnancyhelpnews.com/phc-10-numbers).
5. U.S. Bureau of Labor Statistics, "National Compensation Survey: Employee Benefits in the United States, March 2023," September 2023, https://www.bls.gov/ebs/publications/employee-benefits-in-the-united-states-march-2023.htm.
6. Gallup, "Church Attendance and Party Identification," May 17, 2005, https://news.gallup.com/poll/16345/church-attendance-party-identification.aspx; The Washington Post, "Abortion Rights Advocates Score Major Midterm Victories Across U.S.," November 9, 2022, https://www.washingtonpost.com.

7. Planned Parenthood Federation of America. Planned Parenthood. https://www.plannedparenthood.org/.

Strategy 6

1. Thomas Aquinas, *Summa Theologiae Part II-II, Q. 154, A. 2.*
2. Thomas Aquinas, *Summa Theologiae Part II-II, Q. 10, A. 12.*
3. Thomas Aquinas, *Summa Theologiae Part I, Q. 98, A. 2.*
4. Plato, *Republic, Book VII* (*The Allegory of the Cave*).
5. Aristotle, *Politics, Book VIII.*
6. Saint Augustine, *De Magistro* (*On the Teacher*).
7. Adam Laats, "Our Schools, Our Country: American Evangelicals, Public Schools, and the Supreme Court Decisions of 1962 and 1963," *Journal of Religious History, 36, no. 3* (*2012*): *319–34, at p. 321–22.*
8. "Busting the 'No Money,'" *Texas Policy*, October 2, 2023, https://texaspolicy.com.

Strategy 8

1. James C. Dobson, *Interview with Ted Bundy, recorded January 23, 1989, Focus on the Family, Colorado Springs, CO. Transcript and audio available in Fatal Addiction: Ted Bundy's Final Interview, Focus on the Family, 1989. Archived at https://www.focusonthefamily.com/media/ted-bundy-interview.*
2. Pornhub, "2023 Year in Review," December 14, 2023, https://www.pornhub.com/insights/2023-year-in-review; Laila Mickelwait (@LailaMickelwait), "Prnhub, the world's most popular prn site with 130 million daily users," X post, September 3, 2023, https://x.com/LailaMickelwait/status/1700936145634537844.
3. James C. Dobson, *Interview with Ted Bundy, recorded January 23, 1989, Focus on the Family, Colorado Springs, CO. Transcript and audio available in Fatal Addiction: Ted Bundy's Final Interview, Focus on the Family, 1989. Archived at https://www.focusonthefamily.com/media/ted-bundy-interview* (*accessed March 11, 2025*).
4. Jeffrey Dahmer: The Exclusive Interview, aired February 17, 1993. Transcript published in The Milwaukee Cannibal: Jeffrey Dahmer's Confessions, edited by Robert J. Dvorchak and Lisa Holewa, 143–148, New York: Dell Publishing, 1997.
5. Donald T. Lunde, *The Die Song: A Journey into the Mind of a Mass Murderer* (San Francisco: San Francisco Book Co., 1991), 187–189 (interview conducted April 15, 1991, at California Medical Facility).
6. Joel Norris, *Arthur Shawcross: The Genesee River Killer* (New York: Pinnacle Books, 1992), 234–236 (interview conducted June 12, 1990, at Sullivan Correctional Facility).

7. Jill C. Manning, "The Impact of Internet Pornography on Marriage and the Family: A Review of the Research," testimony before the U.S. Senate Committee on Commerce, Science, and Transportation, November 10, 2005, referencing American Academy of Matrimonial Lawyers, 2002, cited in Marripedia, "Effects of Pornography on Marriage," accessed June 3, 2025, https://marripedia.org/effects_of_pornography_on_marriage.
8. Sara Konrath, "The Empathy Paradox: Increasing Disconnection in the Age of Increasing Connection," in Handbook of Research on Technoself: Identity in a Technological Society, ed. Rocci Luppicini (Hershey, PA: IGI Global, 2013), 204–28, https://doi.org/10.4018/978-1-4666-2211-1.ch012.

Strategy 9

1. International Labour Organization, Walk Free, and International Organization for Migration, Global Estimates of Modern Slavery: Forced Labour and Forced Marriage (Geneva: International Labour Organization, 2022), https://www.ilo.org/publications/global-estimates-modern-slavery-forced-labour-and-forced-marriage.[](https://www.ilo.org/publications/major-publications/global-estimates-modern-slavery-forced-labour-and-forced-marriage)
2. Office of Inspector General (OIG), "ICE Cannot Monitor All Unaccompanied Migrant Children Released from DHS and HHS Custody" (OIG-24-30).
3. Save the Children, "Child Trafficking: Myths vs. Facts," accessed June 3, 2025, https://www.savethechildren.org/us/what-we-do/protection/child-trafficking; International Labour Organization, Walk Free, and International Organization for Migration, Global Estimates of Modern Slavery: Forced Labour and Forced Marriage (Geneva: International Labour Organization, 2022), https://www.ilo.org/publications/global-estimates-modern-slavery-forced-labour-and-forced-marriage.
4. United Nations Office on Drugs and Crime, 2024 Global Report on Trafficking in Persons (Vienna: UNODC, 2024), https://www.unodc.org/unodc/en/data-and-analysis/glotip.html.
5. United States Department of State, 2024 Trafficking in Persons Report (Washington, DC: Department of State, 2024), https://www.state.gov/reports/2024-trafficking-in-persons-report/.[](https://www.state.gov/briefings-foreign-press-centers/2024-trafficking-in-persons-report)
6. Naomi Miles, "Trafficking, Prostitution and Pornography: The Inherent Connections," Christian Concern, November 10, 2020, https://christianconcern.com/comment/trafficking-prostitution-and-pornography-the-inherent-connections/.[](https://christianconcern.com/comment/trafficking-prostitution-and-pornography-the-inherent-connections/)
7. Lora Lucinda, "U.S. Is a Top Destination for Child Sex Trafficking, and It's Happening in Your Community," The Heritage Foundation, July 27, 2023,

https://www.heritage.org/crime-and-justice/commentary/us-top-destination-child-sex-trafficking-and-its-happening-your-community.

8. Catharine A. MacKinnon, "Pornography as Trafficking," 26 Mich. J. Int'l L. 993 (2005), https://repository.law.umich.edu/mjil/vol26/iss4/1.

Strategy 10

1. Thomas Aquinas, *Summa Theologiae II-II, Q. 64, A. 7.*
2. Augustine, *The City of God,* vol. 2, Book 19, ch. 7.
3. Thomas Aquinas, *Summa Theologiae Q. 40, A. 1.*
4. Thomas Aquinas, *Summa Theologiae Q. 94.*
5. Augustine, *Letter 138 (2.13).*

Strategy 11

1. Thomas Aquinas, *Summa Theologiae, Q. 31, A. 3.*
2. Armas, K. (2025, January 31). JD Vance is wrong: Jesus doesn't ask us to rank our love for others. National Catholic Reporter. https://www.ncronline.org/opinion/guest-voices/jd-vance-wrong-jesus-doesnt-ask-us-rank-our-love-others.

Strategy 12

1. Federal Reserve Bank of New York, "Quarterly Report on Household Debt and Credit: Q4 2024," February 12, 2025, https://www.newyorkfed.org; LendingTree, "2025 Credit Card Debt Statistics," May 13, 2025, https://www.lendingtree.com.
2. Congressional Budget Office, "Effects of the Immigration Surge on the Federal Budget and the Economy," July 22, 2024, https://www.cbo.gov/publication/60165.

ACKNOWLEDGMENTS

I am deeply grateful to my wife, Joy, and our eight children, whose steadfast love and support anchor my every endeavor. Your sacrifices and prayers sustain me. My thanks extend to the New Saint Thomas Institute community and my Patreon supporters, whose encouragement and engagement fuel my mission to share truth. I am indebted to the team at Post Hill Press for their dedication in bringing this book to life. To my readers, your enthusiasm for exploring faith, history, and patriotism inspires me daily. Above all, I give glory to God, whose grace guides my pen to proclaim His kingdom in these challenging times.

A SPECIAL THANKS TO OUR LAUNCH TEAM

I am especially grateful to our *Christian Patriot* Launch Team who read the book before publication and also helped us with the promotion. Thank you for your time, work, and enthusiasm.

Colette Abascal, Diana Abbott, Tracy Abbott, Josie Abeyta, Juliet Abraham, Emil Abraham, Sharon Abrahamson, Joseph Abreu, TJ Achatz, Jose Adame, Frank Adamo, Terry Adams, Joseph Adamson, Robyn Adler, Rudy Agresta, Rita Aguilar, John Anthony Aguirre, Armando Aguirre-Jodlowiec, Shaun Ahern, Abelard Aldama, Claudia Alderete, Anil Alexander, Shonda Alexandra, Maria De Las Victorias Alfano, Raymond Aliganyira, Sharon Allan, Cynthia Allen, Jace Allen, Angela Allen, Christopher Allen, Barbara Allen Rosser, Dr. Mikhail Alnajjar, Jorge Alonzo, Teresita Alvarez, Alexis Alvarez Padron, Billy Ames, Jose Amezcua, Audrey Amort, Vincent Amuso, Jean Anderson, Murrey Anderson, Jerehmy Anderson, Benjamin Anderson, Nicole Anderson, Anita Anderson, Jo Reynetta Andonie, Graciela Andrade, Sarrie Andrade, Efe Andrew, Marybeth Anthony, Thomas Antulov, Thomas Antulov, Andrew Apostolik, Cynthia Arias, Karen Arilli, Maria Cristina Ariza-Gomez, Kristy Armas, Stephanie Armbruster, Ed Armendariz, Samantha Armentor, Nathene Arthur, Oscar Artola, Matthew Ashburn, Ellen Auger, Julius Aurelio, Louise Aussant, Doug Austreim, Laura Avenetti, Robert Avery, Robert

Avery, Susana Ayers, James Ayers Jr., Debbie Azevedo, Kristine Azzarello, Philippe Baaklini, Heidi Bach, Ph.D., Jacqueline Badolato, Luke Baierl, Robert Bailey, Roxanne Bailey, Eric Baker, Kate Baker, Marilyn E. Baker, Clara Baker, Evan Bakhet, Shari Bakken, Colletta Bakken, Brian Baldwin, Jatte Baleyos, Nune Balgomera, Brian Ball, James Ballard, Gary Bamber, Ignacio Barba Castro, Daniel Barbaglia, Dina Barbarino, George Barber, Alexander Barber, Kristina Barber, Karinne Barbosa, Deena Barca, Devin Barela, Michael Barker, James Barkey, Ben Barksdale, Tracey Barnes, Thecla Baron, Scott Barone, Tony Barrett, Reniel Barroso, Jenifer Barry, Daniel Barry, Deirdre Barry, Sean Barry, Scott Bartl, Jill Bates, Jacqueline Bates, Bernice Batson, Mary Bayless, Douglas Bayley, Gregory Bazaure, Helen Beabey, Sherry Bean, Scott Beasley, Adriana Beaumont, Robert Becht, Tereza Becica, Mimi Beck, Joshua Beck, Stacey Becker, Fr. Ernest Bedard Ofm Cap., Justin Beirouti, Stephen Beisang, Maria Beisert, Bridgit Bellini, Anne-Marie Bellshot, Joseph Belosic, Chris Benkendorf, Andrew Bennett, James Benoit, Celeste Benson, Gregory Berger, Maggie Bermudez, Jeffrey Bernard, Dan Bernspång, Mary Bernstein-Hintz, Mary Bernstein-Hintz, Monica Berry, Anita Besch, Linda Besink, Laura Bettorf, Brian Beuter, Shelly Beyer, Gerard Biagan, Roger Bienvenu, Amy Biller-Boucher, Paul Binfet, Kathleen Bishop, Robert Black, Maria Elvira Blagrove, Valerie Blandford, Donnie Blankenship, Donna Blasdell, Aleksandra Blaszczyk, Johnathan Blauw, Mark Bleil, Jenelle Blevins, Tracy Boak, Tracy Boak, Richard Bochniewicz, Dr. Suzanne Boese, John Bogensparr, Victor Bohus, Victor Bohus, Mary Boik, Edna Bollman, Carlette Bonnette, Darlene Boos, Mary Bordi, Marita Borer, Carlos Borras, Mike Boschert, Rita Boskovski, Vince Bottoni, Jane Bouck, Patricia Boyd, Linda Boyer, Sherry Bradl, Nancy Brady, Deann Brandel, Joe Brauer, Timothy Braun, Larry Bravo, Joseph Bremer, Marian Brennan, Janet Brennan, Pamela Briddell, Chuck Brinker,

Deb Britain, Marianne Brokaw, Finn Brooke, Rene Brooker, Kenneth Brose, Wesley Brown, Jeffrey Brown, Matthew Brown, Sherri Brown, Carolyn Brown, Dorothy Marie Brown, William Brown III, Robert Browning, Joseph Brozek, Pam Brubaker, Deborah Bruno, Christine Brusnahan, Karen Bryan, Kate Bryan, Miranda Bryant, Mike Bryant, Carol Bryant, Mark Bryant, Marty Buchheit, Maria Budiman, Jan Bugaj, Eduardo Buisson, Linda Bukalski, Pamela Bukowski, Fred Bukowski, Judy Bulcroft, L. Elena Bumb, Michele Bunker, Fran Burazin, Fran Burazin, Vera Burianek, Peter Burke, Kimberly Burke, Elizabeth Busekrus, Sherry Bush, Sherry Bush, Todd Bushee, Martin Butler, Tony Butler, Nicolette Butler, William Butler, David Byers, Michaela Byrnes, Robert Byrns, Eric Cabana, Jennifer Cabrera, Lourdes Cacanindin, Marie Caddell, Elizabeth Calabrese, Theresa Calihan, Mark Calvo, Michael Camacho, Lloyd Camelo, Kevin Campbell, Colleen Campbell, Richard Campbell, Cristina Campos, Kathleen Campos, Diana Cangelosi, Georgia Capozzi, Cathy Carda Schaffer, Rebecca Carey, Colleen Carl, Leo Carling, Christina M. Carlos, Joanne Carlstedt, Marie Carmody, Marie Carmody, Carol Carnese, Dame Carole, Jackie Carpentier, Donna Carret, Richard Carter, Paula Carton, Walter Casler, Andrew F. Castaneda, Kay Castaneda, David Castillo, Jose Antonio Castillo Iniguez, Virginia Castles, Carlos Castro, The People's Catholic, Erin Caudill, Cindy Cazalas, Lawrence Cecchi, MD, Susan Cenci, Sonia Cergnul, Apratim Chakraborty, Tom Chambers, Kechia Chambers, Christopher Chambers, Jerry Chapman, Lisa Chappell, Lisa Charles, Luella Chavez, Brenda Chenal, Maureen Chenette, John Benjamin David Cheuka Tatum, Joseph Chimienti, Josephine Ching'ombe Sr., Prasanth Chinthagada, Alberto Chiquillo, Maria Chirico-Keim, Alex Choong, Jeremy Choquette, Karen Christian, Judy Christopherson, Robert Chufo, Robert Chufo, Alisa Cianciolo, Margaret Clabby, Edward Clancy, Raphaelle Clark, Lenny Claudio, Father Karl Claver,

Father Karl Claver, Barbara Cleary, Patricia Cleary, Timothy Cleary, MD, Rebecca Clemenz, Brigitte Clercx, Brigitte Clercx, Philip Clingerman, Sean Cloonan, Victoria Marie Close, Sonja Cloutier, Amy Coad, Dan Coffey, David Coghlan, Rubi Colchao, David Cole, Damian Colehan, Dreama Colf, Erin Collichio, Lily Colon, Essilevy Colon Nevarez, Janice Colon-Mahoney, Caleb Colson, Christina Columbus, Matthew Commons, Stephen Conlon, Michael Connor, Matthew Connor, John Connor, Kate Connor, Maria Conturbi, Dorothy Conway, Gwynethcook56@gmail.com Cook, Sherry Cook, Fidelina Cooper, Exiquio Cooper-Anderson, Brooke Corbett, Sarah Corkery, Christopher Corleone, Matthew Corrigan, Marisa Ann Corsino, Matthew Cortinas, Jomark Corvite, Christine Costanzo, Wayne Costello, Evan Costello, Monica Costello, Peter Costello, Monica Costello, Betsy Liliana Cote De Bejarano, Lisa Cothran, Diana Couch, Kerma Cox, John Cox, O.p., Jackie Crabtree, Joyce Crandley, Shannon Crapia, Teresa Crichton, Terry Crites, Alberta Crosazzo, Jim Crowley, Linda Crowley, Angel Croyle, Cristito Cruz, Laszlo Csany, Katie Cummings, Father Fergal Cummins, Thomas Cusker, Joseph Cusyk, Brynner D Souza, Daniel D'Agostino, Anthony D'Agostino, MD, John D'Alessandro, Malita D'Souza, Blaine D'Acci Sr., Frankie D'Astoli, Rachel D'Auria, Paul Dabney, Deanna Dabrowski, Peter Dabrowski, Natalie Daedler, Jeffrey L Dagenais, Hani Dagher, David Dahl, Kurt Daichendt, Maria Dalgarno, Michael Dalling, Steve Daly, Bonnie Daly, Gerry Daly, Dani DAngelo, Lisa Daniel, Virginia Danna, MaryGrace Dansereau, Juli Davelli, Jean-Michel David, Theresa Davis, Nancy Davis, Emily Davis, Margaret H Davis, James Davis, Sarah Davis, Sarah Davis, Curtis Davis, Mark Davis, Nina Davisson, Yvonne De Garcia, Enzo De Iulio, Theodora De Vos, Jeramie Dean, Andrea Dean, Jay Dear, Ruth Decarie, Alexis DeLaPaz, Rev. Mr. Armando DeLeon, Joseph Delgado, Chris Delgado, Marialisa Delmare, Ric DelValle, Marsha

Dembosky, Pamela DeMichele, Carolyn Denison, Michael Dennison, Joshua Denny, Joshua Denny, Joshua Denny, Joshua Denny, Joshua Denny, Joshua Denny, Laura Denton, Donald Derozier, Jim DeSart, Barbara Devereau-Bourgeois, Patricia Devine, Karen Devine, Cynthia Devine, Marc Devoid, Marc Devoid, Michael DeWitt, Mr. Zenon Dewmyn, R Patrick Diamond, Barbara Diamond, Rick Diana, Ramona Dias, Elizabeth Diaz, Oscar Diaz, Nate Dibley, Andrea Dick, Stephanie Dietz, Robin DiGiovannantonio, Joseph Dillett, Dante-Christian DiLorenzo, Ken Diman, Steve DiTullio, Richard Dixon, Richard Doherty, Alvy Dolle, Pamela Dolney, Joshua Dolnosich, Paul Dombrowski, Brian Domke, Bobby Donahoo, David Donegan, Deborah Donnelly, Christopher Donnelly, James Doone, Mary Ann Dora, Tracy Doub, Ilona Douglas, Roger Downey, Richard Drake, Michael Driscoll, André Du Mont, Joseph DuBois, Lisa Dudzik, James Dugan, Seaneen Duke, Brianne Duncan, Jacob Duncan, Mark Dunn, Bryan Dunne, Jane Dunne-Brady, Michael Dupuis, Łukasz Durka, Łukasz Durka, Carrie Duryea, Abe Dush, Kevin J.s. Duska Jr., Pam Dwyer, Lucia Dziadul, Shawna Dziedziak, Bryan Eagan, Lynn Eareckson, Darren Easterday, Sharlene Easthope-Harper, Margaret Eastwood, Jason Eberly, Elizabeth Ebertowski, Yvonne Eckhart, Chris Edmonds, Helen Edwards, Samuel Edwards, Tricia Edwards, Jan-Henrik Ehrs, Maroun El Khoury, Rev. Benjamin Elias Ocd, Laura Elizalde, Craig Elliott, Rachel Elliott, Jessica Ellis, Maria Ellis, Molly Emerson, Enyamu Emmanuel, Philip Engle, Thomas Engle, David Englestad, Teresa Engley, Rene Entrata, Nicole Ernest, Rudy Escamilla, Anthony Esgate, Will Estes, Reynaldo Estomata, Ryan Estrada, Mário Eusébio, Caitlin Evans, Edward Evans, Lisa Evers, Carol Ewing, Clara Rachel Eybalin Casseus, Christine Faczak, Elisa Fagundes, Joyce Faith, Rolando Fajilan, Cathy Fakult, Michael Fakult, Daniel Fallon, Kathleen Fanone, Louis-Marie Fardet, Colleen Farghum, Frank Farias, Randall Farmer,

Joyce Farmer, Joyce Farmer, Joyce Farmer, Anne Farrell, Kim Fasser, Grace-Valerie Faubion Schaar, Grace-Valerie Faubion Schaar, Elizabeth Faust, Judi Feather, Dr. Tammy Ann Fecci, Kathleen Federl, Maria Federle, Debbie Fedorovich, Donna-Lou Fennema, Agnelo Fernandes, Roland Fernandez, Amily Fernandez, Tomás Fernández, Deacon George Ferraioli, Victoria Ferraiolo-Madonia, Lee Ferrance, Ydsia Ferrer, Patty Ferris, Jeff Field, Donna Fike, Chris Finkler, Charles Fischer, Judithann Fischer, Andrea Fisher, Susan Fisher, William Flatley, Gregor Flego, Cynthia Fleming, Lisa Flores, Mark Flores, Eduardo Flores, Andrew Foley, Rose Folse, Tracey Fong, Merlyka Fonseca, Ann Marie Fontana, Catherine Fontenot, Catherine Fontenot, Martin Forbes, Patricia Forde, Abraham Forosan, Maria Forte, Judith Fortua Cruz, Rick Fortune, William Foter, Melissa Fountain, Patricia Fowler, Patricia Fraide, Dina Franks, Wayne Freebern, Carolyn French, Marc French, Robert Friedrich, Laure Friesen, Elroy Friesenhahn, Lilyan Frisch, Marie Fullmer, Sandra Fulton, Gabriel Fung, Rose Funovits, Boneeta G, Elizabeth Gabbard, Heather Gaffney, Michael Galbraith, Paul Galdes, Alana Gale-Perry, Jude Galford, Cristina Galliani, Joseph Galvan, Jim Ganther, Vivian Garcia, David Garcia, Paige Garcia, Denise Garcia, Bryan Gardner, Irene Garger, Betty Garnett, Joni Garrett, Ignacio Garro, Kathleen Gaston, Antonio (Tony) Gatto, Jerry And Doris Gatton, Dionne Gaudineer, Robin Gauthier, Martin Gauthier, Jeannine Gauthier, Karli Gedmin, Karli Gedmin, Karli Gedmin, Becky Gehr, Nathan Geier, Teresa Geiselman, Teresa Geiselman, Justin Geldart, Kenneth Gelskey, Robert Gemignani, Natalie Gentry, Elijah George Antony, Matt Germann, Anthony Ghiardi, Anthony Giangiulio, Vince Giarnella, Christina Giles, Stephen Gillon, Kerry Anne Gilowey, Kerry Anne Gimowey, Brian Giovanetti, Dcn. Mark Girardeau, Christopher Giuliano, Suzi Glaze, Suzi Glaze, Jim Gnadinger, Patrick Gnau, Eric Godwin, James (Jim)

Goelz, Rhonda Goforth, Peter Gojcaj, Paula Gomez, Jesus Gomez, Allyson Gomolka, Henry Gonzales, David Gonzales, Patrick Gonzalez, Shannon Gonzalez, J Antonio Gonzalez, Sergio Gonzalez, Alvaro González, Emily Gooch, Jeremy Goodman, Graham Gordon, Luis Gorres, Tristan Gorst, Denise Goss, Jenna Grable, Annette Grady, Heather Gragert, Jodi Grant, Zachary Thomas Graves, Cathy Gray, Kathy Gray, Hope Gray, Lois Grebosky, Francisco Green, Anne Green, Ann Green, Andrew Greeson, Ray Gregorio, Elizabeth Greiner, Chimene Griego, Patricia Griffin, Gregory Griffith, Mary Grimes, Carol Grippo, Kevin Grogan, Colleen Grogan, Robert Groppe, Christopher Grundmeyer, Brigetta Gruzdis, Francine Gryniuk, Deacon Steve Guckin, Renata Guimarães Dias, Colleen Gulish, Frank Gunseor, Sue Gussert, Luis Guzman, Christopher Haacke, Mary Haberer, Teresa Habib, Joanne Hack, Michael Hagan, Ken Hagen, Fred Halazon, Susy Hale, Kasie Haley, Lea Anna Halfmann, Jeremy Nicholas Halim, Kathleen Hall, Laura Hall, Charles Hamel, Timothy Hamel, Mary Hamill, Katie Hancheck, Bill Hancock, Julie Haney, Jim Hanian, Michael Hankinson, Melissa Hanks, Sheelagh Hanly, Jill Hanon, Donna Hanson, Deborah Hanson, Emily Harder Friedl, Sheilagh Hardy, Kathryn Harkey, William Harrell, Franklyn Harris, Brian Harris, Barbara Harrison, Kathryn Harrison, Mary Hart, Michelle Hart, Greg Hartigan, Melissa Hartke, Gary Hartley, Janet Hartmann, Khaled Hashem, Liela Hathaway, Gerard Havasy', Deacon Geoges Hawarian, Rick Hawkins, Ryan Hawn, Ryan Hawn, Michelle Hawrysio, Daniel Hayes, Matthew Hayes, Deborah Haynes, Michael Haynes, Kathryn Heasley Sanchez, Karen Hedge, Andrea Hedrington, Andrew Heekin, Andrew Heekin, Pamela Heffron, William Hegeman, Fr. Richard Heilman, Michaelyn Hein, Thomas Heinrich, Melinda Heisserer, Beth Helton, Teresa Hemphill, Catherine Henderson, Thomas Henderson, Anna Hendrick, Sophie Hendry, Colleen Henion, Dennis Hennessy, Wanda

Henry, Michael Henson, Gilbert G Herbig Sr, Matt Hernandez, Victor Hernandez, Regina Heroux, Sara Herrington, John Herron, Patricia Hershwitzky, Erik Heun, Erik Heun, Joanna Hidalgo, Cindy Hiew, Brigid Higgins, Rebecca Highstreet, Katherine Higuera, Vivian Higuera, Peter Hildebrand, Joshua Hinch, Charles Hines, Carl Hingst, Darlene Hinman, Timothy Hinote, Gianna Hinski, Bernard Hinsley, Jessica Hintermeister, Kevin Hirakis, Paul J. Hiryak, Matthew Hisscock, Patrick Hoage, Martin Hodgins, Gary Hoeger, Matt Hoehn, Teonna Hoffman, Paulette Hoffpauir, Lauren Hoffpauir, Linda Hoffstetter, Thomas Hoflich, John Hohn, Lynn Ellen I Normally Go By "Ellen" Holden, Carol Holder, Mario Holguin, Frances Holmes, Quéva Hombeline, Jan Hong, Patricia Hooten, Michael Hopson, Matthew Horn, Suzanne Horn, Susan Horn-Cherry, John Hotchkin, Julie Howard, Carol Howard, Glen Howard, Rachel Hudson, Sean Hudson, Cindy Huger, Steve Hughes, Mark Hugoboom, Tammy Human, Trever Humphres, Helen Hund, Helen Hund, Michael Hurley, Fr Brian Hurley, Alex Hurtado, Angela Hutton, Peter Hwang, Steve Hyatt, Joseph Iannone, Nate Igielinski, Martin Obinna Ileagu, Conor Imhoff, Sarah Impecoven, Thomas Insall, Salvatore Iorfida, Megan Ippoliti, Nancy Irvin, Pete Isermann, Bryan Istenes, Dale Iurillo, B. C. Iversen Jr., Ryan Jacinto, Gary Jack, Mike Jackson, Anthony Jackson, Michael Jacobazzi, Brayden Jacobs, Kimberly Jacobs, Quirino Jacques, Nancy Jaeger, Flo Jakobeit, Flo Jakobeit, Ewa Jakobson, Arkadiusz Jakubczyk, Jakub Jakubík, David James, Lee Ann Jaramillo, Christopher Jasper, Christopher Jasper, Carmen Jasper, Erwin Jaumann, Maria Paz Jazmines, Karlo Jelincic, Tatiana Jenkins, Desiree Jennings, Arthur Jennings, Désirée Jennings, Désirée Jennings, George Jeruzal, Anita Joce, Darryn Johnnie, Michael Johnoff, Michael Johnoff, Jennifer Johnson, William Johnson, Christa Johnson, Nolan Johnson, Jennifer Johnson, Barry Johnson, Jeff Jones, Walter Jones, Deena Jones, Luke Jones, Audrey

Jones, James Jordan, Robert Joseph Patterson, Angela Joses, Lydia Josipovic, Bradley Jouty, Edith Joyce, Randy Juanta, Maria Judge, Maria Judge, Rodrigo Júlio, Charles Junjulas, James Kachler, Amber Kaelin, Joseph Kalus, Rose Kaniper, Susan Kantarakias, Joseph Karanja, Glenn Karhoff, Victor Karlak Karlak, Steven Katonka, Rita Kay, Debbie Kelly, Norm Kelly, Tuaca Kelly, Kathleen Kelly Wojtkowiak, David Kemp, Sylvia Kendall, Emily Kennedy, Pam Kennedy, Keith Kennedy, Joshua Kenney, Max Keown, Rose Marie Kerner, Gwendolyn Kerr, Chandler Kerr, Dolorese Kershaw, Christopher Kertes, Christopher Kertes, Christopher Kertes, James Kho, Brad Kidd, Reanin Kielmeyer, Alexander Kilates, Lucy Kildow, Mary Kimball-Smith, Kay King, Angelique Kinney, Charmie Kirby, Robert Kirby, Robert Kirk, Robert Kirk, Joshua Kizer, Maureen Klecker, Clinton Kliethermes, Carmen Klocko, Noah Klosinski, Robert Klotz, Bradley Kneeland, Sara Knoble-Sanchez, Paul Koch, Joseph Koechl, Michael Koeniger, Tim Kokesch, Christopher Kollmeyer, Martin Chris Komakech, Martin Chris Komakech, Mike Kooger, Anne Kootz, Kevin Koppmeier, Theresa Koshut, Urszula Kotowska-Walczak, Diana Kovacic, Kristina Kovacs, James Kovats, Zach Krajicek, Molly Kraker, Steve Kraut, Jana Krcek, Randy Krebs, Larry Kreitzer, Julie Krol, Joseph Kruger, James Krupa, Krystyna Krupa, Sabina Kruse, Jeff Krusinski, Tom Kuble, Gary Kujawa, Rita Kukura, Jean L'Olive, Dawn L'Italien, Susan Labadin, Robert Lacey, Dana LaCombe, Lance LaCroix, Rachel LaDavia, Joshua LaFond, Joe Lafuente, Laurie Lalko, Gael Lambie, Laura Lamendola, Mariacristina Lampugnani, Marianne Lan, Joe Landreneau, Carolyn Landry, Katie Lane, Maria Lang, Elisabeth Langenkamp, Candace Langsfeld, Jason Lara, Jason Lara, Scott Larimer, Brenda Laronde, Kris Larsen, Christian Lasval, Nancy Laughlin, Donna Lauritzen, Kathleen Lavalley, Douglas Law, Maryellen Lawrence, Victor Lawrence, Joe Lazar, Julie Lazaro, Kevin Le, Rachel Le Grand, Paul

Leader, Madeleine Leahy, Kimberli Mae Lebens, James LeBert, Tammy LeBleu, Cathy Ledder, C Angel Lee, Wayne Lee, Andrea Lefebvre, Marguerite-Marie Lefranc, James Lehmann, Fiona Lehmberg, Donna Lehr, Kimberly Leipham, Steve Lenz, Fernando Leon-Guiu, Charles Leonard, Dr. Foster Scott Lerner, Dr. Warren Lerner, Michael Lesage, Alex Lessard, Robin Lessard, Mary Lewandowski, Eric Lewis, Elvia Leyva, Rosario Lim, Cody Lindsey, Andrea Llerena, Sara Lloyd, Linda Frances Loch, Mike Lockwood, Catherine Loft, Joshua Logan, David Long, Sandra Lopez, Jonathan Lopez, Janet Lopez, Gabriela Lopez Mijares, Linda Lopp, Yesenia Lopz, Lisa Lottes, Appadoo Louis, Tamara Lourens, Suzanne Love, Samuel Lovely, Ken Lovering, Lucy Lozano Perez, Franciszek Luc, Claudette Lucas, Maileen Lucena, Marvin Lucero, Lizzette Lucero, James Lucier, James Lucier, Ankica Lucin, Maria Lugo, Stephen Lukic, Oscar Rogelio Luna, Christopher Lushis, Jason Luzar, Christopher Lyke, Nichole Lykes, Michael Lyles, Mary Grace Lynch, Michael Lynch, Benjamin Lyng, Tonya Lyons, Taylor Mac Manus, Darryl Macias, Catherine Macmullin, Colm Madden, Patricia Madden, Yvette Mader, Karen Anne Mahoney, Joie Maida, Daniel Maier, Christine Mako, Ernest Maldonado, Cyndy Maletta, Margaret Malina, Kim Mallisee, Daniel Malone, Father Jonathan Malong, Susan Maly, Ekaterina Mamyshev, Ekaterina Mamyshev, Nora Mancuso, Anthony Mancuso, Greg Mandt, Gerard Mangan, Jane Manka, Denise Mantei, Kenneth Manuel, Rev. Leo Marchetti, Maurice Marcus, Samantha Marcus, Charles Marks, Brian Marks, Mychelle Maronde, Kevin Marquess, Vincent Marquez, Claire Marquinez, Catherine Marten, Mary Martin, Corinna Martin, Fernand Martin, Ally Martin, Jorge Luis Martinez, Julie Martinez, Tae Martinez, Martha Martinez, Jose Alejandro Martínez-Castro, Joseph Martyn, Charbel Marun, Joe Marusak, Paul Marvin, Father William Mary, Father William Mary, Daniel Masullo, Karen Mata,

May Matar, May Matar, Jennifer Mathews, Bob Matters, Aduzinda Matthews, Judith Maucieri, Muke Richard Mayoyo, Kay Mc Cabe-Moore, Angela McAfee, Patrick McAvoy, Bradley McBride, John McBride, Donal McCann, Michael McCann, Patricia McCarron, Kevin McClements, Sharon McConlogue, Thomas McCormack, Mariana McCroskey, Jay McCurdy, Frank McDermott, Nicole McDonell, Jody McDonough, Marta McFeeture, Sylvia McGannon, Patricia McGee, Raymond McGlew, Stephen McGuire, Miles McGuire, David McGuire, Dani McHantaf, Dion McInnis, Kenneth McKechnie, John McKenna, Matthew McKibben, Rhonda McKinney, Martin McKinnon, Clancy McQuigg, Ami McSorley, Marc Meadows, Eva Medina, Joseph Medina, Joseph Medina, Nora Medina, Jorge Medina, Dereck Mejias, William Melancon, Ivan Melchor, Miguel Melendrez, Nathy Melgoza, Janice Melhorn, Katherine Mendoza, Maria Milagros Menendez, Mischelle Mercado, Mariette Mercier, Teri Merkle, Kathleen Merry, Bill Mertka, Jenni Mesa-Johnson, Deborah Metcalf, Walter Metrick, Pamela Jean Meyer, June Meyers, Marlene Meza, Martin Micenec, Mark Michalski, Juan Mijares, Rob Mik, Catherine Milanowski, Jennifer Milius, Stephen Miller, Jennifer Miller, John Keehan Miller, Joseph Miller, L Miller, Linda Miller, Taylor Miller, Herschel Millis, Mary Mills, Shari Millspaw, Michael Minges, Dennis Minnice, Joshua Minton, Timothy Misencik, Dolores Mitchell, Donna Mitzel, Cheri Mobley, Piper Mohl, Piper Mohl, Erik Mojica, Judy Moldenhauer, Jonathan Molik, Timothy Moline, Mike Molitor, Jerome Monaco, Parick Monaghan, Ànally Monárrez, Laura Montagano, David Montague, David Montes, James Montgomery, Pam Moore, Christie Moore, Terry Moore, Allison Moore, Xenia Moos, Jorge Mora, Sophia Morais, Danilo Morales, Teresa Morales, Ricardo Morales, Jeffrey Moran, Angela Moreno, Dione Moreno, Daniel Moreno Pons, Michelle Morgan, Annette Moris, Ana G Morquecho, Joe Morrione, Elaine Morris,

Lucy Mosca, Parker Moseley, Deacon Larry Motyka, Florent Morice Mtuka, Eric Mueller, Shirley Muhleisen, Joseph Mularczyk, Umberto Mulè Stagno, Maria Mullins, Yadira Muñoz-Diaz, Nancy Murbach, Elaine Murphy, Aidan Murphy, Brian Murphy, Annie Murphy, Cindy Murphy, James Murray, Andrew Musano, Brian Musha, Kyle Mussmann, Madeleine Myers, Mary Mytnik, Jennifer Nacole, Lisa Nadeau, Gerri Namuth, Bernard Nance, Charlie Naranjo, Sr., Michael Narges, Michael Narges, Leonardo Nascimento, Javier Ñaupari, Ashley Neely, Andrew Neff, Michelle Nelli, Peter Nelson, Keith Nelson, Leilani Nemeroff, Belinda Ness, Jera Neumann, Charles Newman, Todd Newman, Alvin Newton, Joseph Nguyen, Cynthia Nicaud, Debra Nichols, Tracie Nickley, Nicole A. Nieto Quiñonez, MD, Angel Nieves Garcia, Margaret Nikel, Dr Keith Nilsen, John Nimlo, Dalia Nino, Frank Niro, Deb Noel, Seth Noorzad, Vernon Noronha, Sally Norwich, Tom Nosker, Brian Novotny, Michael Noyes, Noelle Nugent, Juan Nunez, Patricia O'Brien, Joe O'Connor, Jonathan O'Connor, Hester O'Donnell, Miriam O'Donoghue, Joanne O'Neill, Joanne O'Neill, Holly O'Bert, Joseph O'Boyle, Robert O'Brien, Darlene O'Connell, Brian O'Curran, Mark O'Kane, Joe O'Neil, Tim O'Brien, Frank O'Brien, Mar Y Ocello, Daniel Ochs, Thomas Odle, Laura Odom, Alexander Ofner, Linda Ofstead, Ubaldo Olague, Michele Olivier, Mary Ollinger, Orlando Olmo, Oscar Olqgue, Karen Olson, Kathleen Ondracek, Katherine Oneill, Gabriele Oogjen, Barbara Opperman, Luis R Oquendo, Lance Orchid, Orlando Orochena Jr, Antonio Orozco, David Ortiz, Raymond Ortiz, Aileen Osias, John Ostermann, Janet Otto, Martin Owens, Mary Pablo, Joyce (Josephine) Pace, Len Pacek, Lupe Padilla, Rebecca Padley, Fr. Nicholas Pagano, Sir Randy Pietro Pagnotta, Natalie Paige, Martin Palacios, Mark Angelo Palomares, Alexander Palyo, Michael Pant, Wolfgang Panzenell, Marc Papa, Drew Pape, Martha Paquin, Patricia Parma, Nanette

Parratto-Wagner, Kristina Parry, Ginger Parten, Tomasz Pasiut, Carol Ann Passante, Joseph Mark Passante, Trey Passman, Rolland Patrick, Ann Patry, Anne Patterson, Erin Patterson, Marie Paul, Joe Paul, Andrew Paul, Susan Pautler, James Pavlick, Ed Pawlak, Tracy Pearson, Bob Pearson, Bob Pearson, Rebecca Peck, Francisco Pedraza, Jr., Alan Peffley, Nives Peharda, Nives Peharda, Ernesto Pelayo, Carlos Pena, Jose Pena, Rudolph Penaranda, Michelle Pendergrass, Emilio Perea, Lorna Pereira, Graciela Perez, Andrew Perez, Pat Perez, Francisco José Pérez Valero, Javier Perezcrespo, Linda Perry, John Peters, Trish Peterson, Nathalie Petruzzelli, Andreas Pfenniger, Amanda Pflanz, Mitzi Phalen, Mariana Phalen, Payton Phalen, Leslie Philip, Carlton Phillips, Denise Phillips, Andrea Phyrillas, Michelle Piccione, George Piccone, Mareda Pierce, Teddy Pierce, Cathy Pierson, Jo Pike, Theresa Pilkerton, Luis Pina, Jorge Pinargotte, Kiki Pinem, Maureen Pinho, Nicholas Pinho, Massimo Pinto, Gayle Piron, Jr Pisula, Amanda Pizzo, John Platt, Hart Ponder, Regina Pontes, Brian Pooley, Christina Poopatana, Kimberly Popovic, Tony Porcaro, Rev. Fr. J. Marcel Portelli, Thomas Pospiech, Patricia Postiglione, Renee Poudrier, Eileen Powell, Dawn Powell, Cathy Powell, Edward Power, Anne Powers, David Powers, Camron Preciado, Dolores Priego-Porras, Bayu Prima, Anthony Primiani, Ervin Prince, Mario Prince, Ervin Prince, Ryan Pritchard, Kent Pritchard, Donna Procher, Jan Prorok, Jan Prorok, Victor Pruchniewski, Luz Prukop, Rachel Pruneau, Cesar Puentes, Quinton Puleo, Quinton Puleo, Eduardo Pulido, Cesar Pulido, Stephen Pulkrabek, Mariya Pullin, Judith Purdom, Jamie Purnell, Toni Pusich, Maddie Putrino, Kenneth Queen, Mauricio Quijada, Conor Quincey, Sue Quinn, Eamonn Quinn, Rafael R. M. Oliveira, Jennifer Racey, Tim Raczek, Christopher Rainbow, Cecilia Ralson, Lino Ramirez, Santiago Ramirez, John Ramirez, Nelson Ramos, Alicia Ramos, Guillermo Ramos, Akinna Ransom, Jeff Rapp, Maria Rapp,

Melko Rasica, James Rauch, Dr. Antone Raymundo, James Redington, Kathleen Reed, Sophie Reen, Jane Refalo, Nathan Reffitt, Mark Reid, Tad Reida, Erin Reilley, Joseph Reilly, Vickie Reinhardt, Bryan Reinholdt, Jr., James Rew, Jeannette Reyes, John Reyher, Adam Rezac, Anne Rhodes, Matthew Ribarich, Gabrielle Rice, Lane Richardson, Cristopher Rico, Bridget Riedell, Sharon Riffle, Jonathan Riley, Michael Riopel, Miranda Rios, Sandee Risner, Teresa Ritchie, Teresa Ritchie, Dr. Lorena Rivarola-Duarte, Eugenio Rivera, Skip Rivers, Murrell Rizon, Jennifer L Roberts, John Roberts, Elizabeth Roberts, Tina H. Roberts, Chris Roberts, Tony Robertson, Susan Robinson, Robert Robinson, Araceli Robinson, Robert Robinson, Alessandra Rocco, Claudio Rocha Dias, Joleen Rocks, Christopher J Rodacy Jr, Delyse Rodrigues, Christine Rodrigues, Frank Rodriguez, Raul Rodriguez, Teresa Rodriguez, Angelica Rodriguez, Karen Rodriguez, Juan Rodriguez, Carlos Rodriguez, Carlos Rodriguez Lampon, Martha Rodriguez Sevillano, Dawn Roeder, Robert Roesser, Matthew Roessner, Mac Rojo, Ilia Roldan, Damon Roman, Patricia Rondeau, Richard Rooney, Lourdes Rosales, Neville Rosario, Eamonn Rosbotham, Amy Rose, Devin Rose, Sharon Rose-Jimenez, Amina Rosen, Katie Rosenshein, Lydia Roskey, Steve Rossi, Kathy Rossi, Michael Rosteet, Darrin Rousse, Andrea Rowe, Sebastián Daniel Rozenblit Vazquez, Patricia Ruba, Maria Rubio, Barbara Ruden, Michael Ruffino, Paul Ruggles, Fernando Ruiz, Adrian Rusch, Linda Ruschak, Brendan Ryan, Linda Ryan, Nelly S, Dilan Saavedra, Bruce Sabalaskey, Daniel Sacino, Maria Sadowski, H. William Safford, Remegio Sagarino, Gilbert Saint Mart, Elisabetta Sala, Adam Salas, Desiree Salas, Sylvia Salas, Shelly Salas-Selem, Dr. Yolanda Salazar, Dereck Saldanha, Dekendrick Samuel, Roy San Buenaventura, Noel Sanabria, Paul Sanchez, Al Sanchez, Maria Sanchez, Julieta Sanchez A, Theresa Sander, Geraldine Sanders, Benjamin Sandoval, Angelo Sandoval, Juan Santana, Fernando

Santos, Alfie Chip Santos, Roland Santos, Liz Santos, Patricia Santy, Austin Sarabia, Michele Sarrazin, Joseph Sarro, Dcn Gabriel Saucedo, Jeremy Sauer, Daniel Sauerwein, Mary Saum, Rose Savage, Deborah Savage, Theresa Saville, John Savin, Rich Scanlon, Stephen Scarallo, Jane Schaal, Jeffrey Schack, Kevin Schad, Angela Schade, Joshua Schaefer, Ernesto Schafran, Mary Schaub, Mary Schaub, Mary Scheetz, Susan Scheibel, Bill Scheible, Gerry Scheidhauer, Patty Schelfhout, James Schiavo, Anastasia Schiele, Jessica Schlick, Christopher Michael Schmitz, Joan Schmutz, Sven Schneider, Eric Schneider, Chad Schockemoehl, Catherine School, Rick Schrader, Michael Schrampf, Brian Schreiber, Michelle Schwab, Christian Schwalb, Catherine Schwant, Stan Schwieterman, Andrew Scollick, Jeffrey Scott, Amanda Scott, Lisa Scrimenti, Craig Scurato, Ashley Seals, Katherine Seastrunk, Pedro Sebastian II, Tod Sedgwick, F Scot Segesman, Ana Seibert, Benjamin Semah, David Seng, Marilyn Seramur, Elisabetta Serrani, Paul Serwinski, Michael Sewchok, Melissa Seymour, Lesa Shackleford, Matthew Shaddrix, Russell Shaffer, Mary K Shanahan, Robert Shannon, Sean Sharer, Kevin Sharpe, Stephanie Shaw, Genie Shaw, Lisa Shea, Robert Shea, Remarna Sheehan, Elizabeth Sheehy, Grant Sheely, Flora Sheldrake, Thomas Shellenberger, Daniel Sherban, Jim Sherbundy, Al Shiya, Ronald Shpakoff, Michael Shurtleff, Kathryn Sibley, Kenneth Siemsen, Marijo Siepierski, Deborah Siff, Suzanne Siguenza, Anderson Silva, John Anthony Silva, Duarte Silveira, Kristin Simmons, Jason Simpson, Lori Sims, Seth Sinclair, Mary Singh, Jeffrey Siu, Annette Skibinski, Wendy Skroska, Brian Slaby, Tristan Slagle, Brenda Sleep, Kate Sloan, Karen Small, Alyssa Smeltzer, Dorothy Smith, Karen Smith, Julie Smith, Gigi Smith, Jeffrey Smith, Bob Smith, Bonnie Smith, Patricia Marie Smith, Kathy Smith, Matthew Smith, Kolton Smith, Joseph Smith, Karen Smith, Loretta J. Smith aka Loretta Warner, Dr. Karen Smith Gallo, Paul Smithard,

Pavel Smolko, Valerie Smyder, Linda Snobl, Vasco Soares, Arlene Somers, Henh Ban Song, Ivan Šop, Patrick Sordelet, Constancio Soto, Arnoldo Soto, Tatiana Souza, Carole Souza, Karen Spaziante, Larry Spencer, Charles Spivak, Patricia Spoerl, Marcell Spohn Wright, Priscilla Sprague, Jack Spring, Jack Spring, Sarah Sprunger, Burke Squires, John Standifird, Brian Standridge, Suzanne Stanton, Kevin Stanton, Mark Staples, Zoe Starr, John Stastny, Warren Steele, Liam Steinour, Amanda Stephen, Jennifer Stephens, Sandra Stephens, Yvonne Stephenson, Nicholas Steven, Timothy Stevens, Christopher Stevens, Ashley Stinnett, Jesss Stinson, Gabriela Stockton, Elaine Storrs, William Stowe, William Stowe, Scot Stratton, Soraya Strobach, Kyle Strong, Maria Struik, Wendy Strycula, Darwin Stupka, Jacqueline Stutmann, Gustavo Suarez, Joseph Subjak, Sharon Subjak, Mary Sullivan, Pauline Sultana, Sandi Sultanowsky, Scott Sutherland, Simon Sutton, Kalsoom Sutton, Karl Svensen MD, Edward Swann III, Jon Swecker, Susan Sweeney, Corey Swope, Tabatha Sword, Denis Sychev, Sean Sylvester, Jan Szafranski, Doug Szot, Claudia T, Chelly Bautista Tabaloc, Janet Tabinski, Alice Talbot, Ashley Tamburrino, Lara Tancock, Karen Taraborelli, Sr. Miryam Taranée, Andrew Taylor, Jeff Taylor, Sheila Taylor, Katarina Teburcia, Earl Teeter, Colette Tellman, Guadalupe Tenpenny, Marianna Thelen, Pravin Thevathasan, Pravin Thevathasan, Philip Thoma, Jobe Thomas, Cathryn Thomas, Teresa Thompson, John Thompson, Kyle Thompson, John Thompson, David Thrower, Ross Ticknor, Michael Tillar, Cindy Titus, Philip Todd, Anna Tognaci, Austin Tomasone, Karole Toney, Ailish Topf, Greg Torres, Robert Torres, Robert Torres, Joli Toth, Claude Touchette, Dr. Kristin Towle, Samuel Towne, Tony Townsell, Brian Trahan, Brian Trahan, Ray Trainque, Ian Trammell, PhD, Lucas Trapani, Janet Trapp, Theresa Trautwein, Vincent Treacy, Josie Trejo, Mark Trieger, Hao Trinh, Joseph Trombello, Mary Truckenmiller, Richard True, Lois

Tucci, Gary Tucker, James Tucker, Nedra Tuller, Randolph Tupas, Michele Turley, Rebecca Turner, Joseph Turner, Jakub Tuzinsky, Mary Ulander, Darin Underhill, Nathan Urban, Mary Urbanski, Katherine Urquidi, Rosanna Utter, Clark Edward Uytico, Brian Vacha, Lima Vadakara, Pam Vaillancourt, Deborah Valdez, Charlotte Valencic, Dr. Lisa Van Bramer, Teo Van Der Weele, Paul Vandenheede, Patricia Vanderloo, Jennifer Vanderveer, Gary Vanhorn, Matthew VanWormer, Germaine Vany, Alan Varagona, Liz Varela, João Vasconcelos, Jorge Vasquez, Andrew Vassiliou, Joanne Vavoso, Luis Vazquez, Lee Veinot, Andrej Veletic, Angel Velez, Michael Velosa, Philip Vera, Josh Verdin, Benjamin Verhovsek, Patricia Verlander, Michael Vernon, Edgar Vigil, Rose Villegas, Gabriel Villegas, Joseph Vincent, Jan Vis, Brian Vista, Joyce Vitalo, Benjamin Vogel, Guy Vogrin, Charles Volz, Ryan Vonderhaar, Marlin Vrbas, John Vrla, David Wagner, Patricia Wagner, Matt Wagner, Gina Wagner, Thommy Wagner, Anthony Waguespack, Jesse Waitz, Heather Walker, Hilary Walker, Messina Walkling, James Walsh, Julia Walters, Frances Walters, Jeff Walton, Catherine Walton, Barbara Wanamaker, Todd Wannemuehler, Christina Wanser, Joseph Wantz, David Warner, Kenneth Warnshuis, Charles Warwick, Marie Washburn, Merijule Washington, Bill Watercutter, Kelly Wathen, Cordelia Watkins, Father Melvin Watts FSSP, Tonchi Weaver, Marianna Webber, Andrew Weber, Janell Weber, Gianna Weber, Brian Weber, Misty Weber, Deborrah Wegmann PhD, Dominik Węgrecki, Tim Weiland, Mary Weinheimer, John Weiser, Michael Welle, James Wellman, Marissa Wellman, Mike Wenger, Christopher Wentling, Cory Whatley, Mary-Lynn Wheatley, Kathleen White, Barry White, Karen White, Patricia Whittier, Joseph Whitty, Joseph Whittyluna, Steven Wiberg, Gary Wiley, Mary Williams, Joshua Williams, Roxine Williams, Fredrick Williams, Marie Williams, Donna Williams, Deanna Williston OFS, David Wills, JB Willson, Nita Wilson, Gerard

Wilson, Stephen Wilson, James Wilson, Kyle Wirachowsky, Debbie Wirt, Joe Witherell, John Wolfe, Tim Wolfe, Travis Wolff, Tres Wolfford, Ken Wondra, Eileen Wood, Russell Wooten, Georgina Work, Jasmine Worsham, Jordan Wright, Erika Wright, Thomas Wroblewski, Anasetasia Wulf, Andreas Wurm, Fin Wycherley, Lawrence Wynja, George Xerri, Amanda Yates, Andrew Yeager, Nancy Yen Chong, James Yonkers, David Young, Edward Young, Martha Young, Julis Young, Elisabeth Young, David Yung, Christian Zacarias, Joe Zamora, Marilyn Zayac, Andrew Zenchak, Nina Zetty, Phillip Zezulak, Kathleen Ziems, Brent Zimmerman, Thomas Ziolkowski, David M. Zuber, Bryan Zumbaugh, Madalene Zwick, and Andrzej Zyla.

In Christ,
Taylor R. Marshall